LOOKING WEST

LOOKING WEST

REGIONAL TRANSFORMATION AND THE FUTURE OF CANADA

LOLEEN BERDAHL AND ROGER GIBBINS

UNIVERSITY OF TORONTO PRESS

Library and Archives Canada Cataloguing in Publication

Berdahl, Loleen, 1970– , author
Looking West : regional transformation and the future of Canada / Loleen Berdahl, Roger Gibbins.

Includes bibliographical references and index.
Issued in print and electronic formats.

ISBN 978-1-4426-0875-7 (bound).—ISBN 978-1-4426-0645-6 (pbk.).—
ISBN 978-1-4426-0646-3 (pdf).—ISBN 978-1-4426-0647-0 (epub)

    1. Canada, Western—Economic policy.   2. Canada, Western—Politics and government. 3. Regionalism—Canada, Western.   4. Federal-provincial relations—Canada, Western. I. Gibbins, Roger, 1947– , author   II. Title.

HC117.W3B47 2014 338.9712   C2013-906155-X   C2013–906156–8

We welcome comments and suggestions regarding any aspect of our publications—please feel free to contact us at news@utphighereducation.com or visit our Internet site at www.utppublishing.com.

North America
5201 Dufferin Street
North York, Ontario, Canada, M3H 5T8

2250 Military Road
Tonawanda, New York, USA, 14150

ORDERS PHONE: 1–800–565–9523
ORDERS FAX: 1–800–221–9985
ORDERS E-MAIL: utpbooks@utpress.utoronto.ca

UK, Ireland, and continental Europe
NBN International
Estover Road, Plymouth, PL6 7PY, UK

ORDERS PHONE: 44 (0) 1752 202301
ORDERS FAX: 44 (0) 1752 202333
ORDERS E-MAIL: enquiries@nbninternational.com

Every effort has been made to contact copyright holders; in the event of an error or omission, please notify the publisher.

This book is printed on paper containing 100% post-consumer fibre.

The University of Toronto Press acknowledges the financial support for its publishing activities of the Government of Canada through the Canada Book Fund.

Printed in Canada

RECYCLED
Paper made from
recycled material
FSC® C103567

To Katie, Zoë, and Dara

Contents

Figures and Tables

Acknowledgements

LOLEEN BERDAHL: WRITING *LOOKING WEST* has been a great pleasure. I spent my early career as a researcher at the Canada West Foundation, and in my decade there I developed a strong appreciation of western Canada, its history, and its potential. I also deepened my passion for public policy, socio-economic data, and intergovernmental relations. Since joining the University of Saskatchewan in 2008, I have extended my examination of these themes, and western Canada continues to fascinate me. *Looking West* has allowed me to consider the West at length, a most interesting and enjoyable exercise.

I have been particularly grateful that *Looking West* provided me the opportunity to again work on a major project with my co-author Roger Gibbins. Writing with Roger is always a wonderful experience, and *Looking West* has been particularly so.

Thank you to Meritt Kocdag, Sara Waldbillig, and Kelton Doraty for your excellent research assistance, to Robert Roach and Todd Hirsch for your insights and suggestions, to the blind reviewers who provided constructive and valuable feedback, to my colleagues at the University of Saskatchewan, and to the University of Toronto Press—particularly Michael Harrison—for your support of the book.

A special thank you to my family for all of your love and support. My daughters, Katie and Zoë, are a daily inspiration.

ROGER GIBBINS: *LOOKING WEST* is a major milestone in a long personal journey to come to grips with the rich history, contemporary realities, and future potential of western Canada. Since joining the University of Calgary in 1973 I have been trying to move beyond my formative childhood experiences in northern British Columbia to embrace the broader western region that was at best a vague abstraction when I was growing up. My colleagues at the University of Calgary were hugely important in helping me come to grips with the West and, more particularly, with its place in Canada. Most of my academic work focused on the complex relationship between the West and the rest, and in this endeavour I was helped enormously by my friends and colleagues at the University of Calgary.

The depth and breadth of my understanding were then strengthened through 14 years as president of the Canada West Foundation. Every year, indeed almost every day, my colleagues at the Foundation stretched my understanding and filled in so many holes. Here I owe special thanks to the 50 or 60 directors of the Foundation that I came to know and respect. Throughout the 14 years, they added the nuance and regional breadth that a BC kid working in Calgary too often lacked. They also helped me move from a focus on regional grievances to a sense of optimism and opportunity. Their remarkable lives were a constant inspiration, convincing me that the best was yet to come. In so many ways, it is their insights and passion that I have brought to *Looking West*.

My thanks, of course, extend to my co-author Loleen who provided so much of the motivation and heavy lifting for this project. Her gentle stewardship was brought to bear throughout when my chapter drafts drifted away from hard evidence to something approaching poor poetry.

Finally, *Looking West* is about the future of this dynamic part of Canada, and here my granddaughter Dara has given me an important stake in that future. The West's vast potential is hers to seize.

Introduction

Continuity and Change in the Canadian West

Some of the most striking images of western Canada reflect the region's timeless geography. A prairie landscape that can seem both empty and endless, the "miles and miles of miles and miles" often used to describe Texas but more appropriately used to describe the Canadian prairies. The fields of wheat and canola stretching to a horizon so distant as to be almost invisible. The Rockies and their aura of untamed, even untamable wilderness. The rugged coast and rain forests of British Columbia—a landscape of transcendent beauty painted by incessant rain. These images, however, can mistakenly suggest a region locked in time and space, and nothing could be farther from the truth. More recent images draw our attention to a natural environment that is more vulnerable than untamed, the massive industrial development of the oil sands in Alberta and natural gas deposits in British Columbia, almost boundless resource wealth precariously linked to global markets, and a human landscape that is emphatically urban rather than rural. The prairie exodus during the dust bowl of the Great Depression has been replaced by steady in-migration from other parts of Canada and the world. British Columbia is less at the margins of national life and more at the cutting edge of a global economy increasingly dominated by Asia.

Our focus in the chapters that follow is on how all of the above have shaped the *political landscape* of western Canada, and here we encounter patterns of both continuity and change. The continuity comes through strong voices of political protest often laced with the passion and utopian optimism of religion; through a boom-and-bust economy that busted as much as it boomed; through British Columbians, who are only loosely tethered to the national community, fighting their unique demons of class and populist politics; and, of course, through the ongoing efforts of self-defined outsiders struggling for respect and power at the centre of Canadian political life, a struggle encapsulated in the Reform Party's mantra "The West wants in." This cacophony of protest has done so much to define the region and, somewhat ironically, to place it outside the Canadian mainstream. And yet now the aspirations and frustrations that animated western discontent over the years have been replaced by the new reality: the West is in, and many of the levers of national economic and political power rest in western Canadian hands. The protest tradition has yielded, perhaps to everyone's surprise, a dynamic region that leads rather than reacts to national economic, social, and political change.

Today, everything seems to be tipping to the West—the economy, population growth and immigration, wealth, political power, and even hockey as four of Canada's seven NHL teams are now in the western region. This process of widespread incremental change, we argue, has taken Canada to a "tipping point" of the kind described so powerfully by Malcolm Gladwell (2000). More specifically, we use Gladwell's evocative term to refer to the accumulation of incremental change to the point where change suddenly becomes transformative rather than incremental. In a very important sense, the West is no longer the same, and thus neither is the country. Change has overtaken continuity, and although the outlines of the future remain unclear, the construction that is under way both builds upon and goes beyond the foundation of a protest past. In many ways, the West is like the dog that, to its own amazement, has caught the bus after chasing it for years. Now what? How can the opportunity for national leadership be realized?

Our task is to bridge these images of the past, present, and future so we can explain how current political developments in western Canada are deeply rooted in the past while at the same time transcending that past by offering a new Canadian vision. We will sort through a complex history that spans more than a hundred years, four very different provinces, and the loosely knit regional community that encompasses all four. In so doing we will tackle the demographic and economic drivers of political transformation, highlighting changes that by themselves are incremental rather than revolutionary, but when taken together constitute a more fundamental transformation. In this sense, we will challenge William Shakespeare's contention in *The Tempest* that "what's past is prologue," arguing instead that the recent transformation in western Canada has been so dramatic that it constitutes a new reality unbounded by the grievances of the past, or at least offers up that possibility. The West once again offers a blueprint for Canada's future, just as it did at the turn of the twentieth century when the flood of immigrants into western Canada permanently changed the nature of the country.

In many ways our analysis complements the recent work by Darrell Bricker and John Ibbitson, *The Big Shift: The Seismic Change in Canadian Politics, Business and Culture and What It Means for Our Future* (2013). We agree that the economic, cultural, and political map of Canada has been redrawn by transformative forces largely although not exclusively centred in western Canada. Where we are more cautious than Bricker and Ibbitson, and perhaps surprisingly so given our strong western Canadian roots, is with respect to the durability of this "big shift." Here our concern is not with the partisan durability of that shift—national governments will come and go, as they should. Rather, we are concerned with the awesome challenges that confront an export-driven resource economy in a rapidly changing global economy. We are also concerned with the internal coherence of a region facing dramatic challenges related to Aboriginal peoples, resource extraction, market access, environmental protection, and urban design.

Caveats and Limitations

Ours is an ambitious undertaking that covers a great deal of history and geography. In tackling all of this we will draw from but undoubtedly fail to adequately summarize a vast and rich literature on western Canadian politics and on the relationship between the West and Ottawa. To paraphrase Isaac Newton, "If we have seen further it is only by standing on the shoulders of giants." Our contribution to the existing literature will be to move the regional story forward in time and space, an undertaking shaped by our own backgrounds, interests, and limitations.

This book reflects a deep personal engagement with the West; our respective careers and lives have spanned British Columbia, Alberta, and

Saskatchewan, and our scholarly work, in part through the Canada West Foundation, has embraced the region as a whole. This deep and long-standing academic and personal engagement with western Canadian political life means that we will draw explicitly, but sometimes only implicitly and unintentionally, on material that we have published earlier, separately or jointly. We apologize for any inadvertent plagiarism of our own work.

Our West, like our lives and research histories, spans Manitoba, Saskatchewan, Alberta, and British Columbia, but does not extend to the northern territories. In many ways, this separation of the West and the North is artificial and unfortunate as the territorial economies are tightly integrated with the broader western Canadian economy, and the western premiers and their territorial counterparts now meet regularly through the Western Premiers' Conference. Nonetheless, appropriating the North into our discussion of the West would be offensive to many in the North, would greatly outstrip our own knowledge and experience, and would verge upon academic imperialism by western Canadian scholars. In the future, however, there is no question that the interface between western and northern Canada should and will receive much greater attention.

We are both policy wonks through and through, interested in how public policy can be harnessed to regional goals and aspirations. We will therefore focus repeatedly on how provincial and federal public policy might be better aligned with western aspirations. We are not proposing a national policy agenda uniquely tailored to western Canadian interests but rather one that better reflects those regional interests, *and does so in the broader national interest.*

Although this is primarily a book about politics, it is written by political scientists in the earlier spirit of political economy. The analysis draws heavily from economic materials without, hopefully, offending our economist colleagues or mystifying students in political science. That said, some readers may be surprised by the fact that we have not neatly separated or sequenced the economic and political analysis. The explanation is that economic discontent has been so fundamental to political discontent in the West that separation is all but impossible. Just as it would be impossible to write a political history of the United Kingdom without turning repeatedly to the impact of social class, a political history of the United States without turning again and again to race, an Australian history without repeated reference to the transportation of convicts, or a Canadian history without repeated references to language and religion, we found it impossible to pigeonhole our economic analysis. The campaign advice that Bill Clinton kept on his desk throughout the 1996 American presidential campaign applies to our own work: "It's the economy, stupid!" Therefore, economic and political themes are interlaced throughout.

The importance of economics is underscored by occasional comparisons between western Canadian discontent and the nationalist movement in Quebec, contrasting the "West wants in" with "Quebec wants out." The former is not driven by a distinctive regional language, religion, or culture; few see the West as a "distinct society" and western Canadians have sought greater integration into the Canadian society at large, albeit on their own terms. Yes, cultural differences between the West and the rest are often noted, but these have not been significant drivers of regional discontent; they add only colour and spice to a much larger stew. The primary driver of regional discontent has been a long history of national economic policy that has failed to adequately reflect, or is believed to have failed to reflect, western Canadian interests and aspirations. This core of economic discontent is quite different from the nationalist movement in Quebec, and it has led in turn to a regional political critique that is again quite different from political critiques embedded in the nationalist movement.

In one way or another, Quebec nationalists have sought to have more power and constitutional responsibilities vested in the Quebec National Assembly and less in Ottawa, even to the point of calling for an independent Quebec. Western Canadians have been far more exorcised about how power is executed in Ottawa and have not, with some exceptions, promoted any massive migration of constitutional authority from Ottawa to the provincial capitals. There has long been an assimilationist impulse in western Canada, one that arose from the need of a frontier society to assimilate a very diverse and polyglot immigrant population. On this front, language politics in the West and Quebec inevitably collided as the constitutional protection of the French language was often seen as an unwelcome shield behind which other and, in the prairie context, much larger ethnic groups might seek protection from assimilationist pressure. It was, and is, very difficult to reconcile this approach to linguistic minorities with the historical protection of the French language within a bilingual Canada.

There is nothing surprising in the observation that the Quebecois and western Canadians have promoted very different national visions. Nor is it surprising that competing visions from Quebec dominated national debate for most of the post-war period, at least from the 1960s to the early years of the twenty-first century. What may be more surprising is the tenacious character of western Canadian visions forged by the frontier experience, the success they have enjoyed in Canada's constitutional odyssey, and the extent to which they will have even greater traction in the years to come.

What Lies Ahead

The book begins with chapter 1, which places a greater emphasis on continuity than change as it explores western Canada's protest tradition. The discussion rotates around the perceived need for the political reform of parliamentary institutions, including the political parties that populate those institutions, and ultimately around the need for national economic policy that more adequately reflects western interests and aspirations. The chapter, however, is more than a litany of populist complaints; it makes the case that it is possible to extract from the western Canadian protest tradition a new national vision for Canada in new global circumstances. It would be a mistake to focus on the negative western Canadian voice, on the protest and grievances, to the neglect of the positive voice. Western Canadians and their political leaders have been far more than whiners and malcontents; they have also been visionaries about their region, and about Canada.

Chapter 2 then sets the stage for an understanding of change by describing significant patterns of demographic transformation taking place with respect to both the West and the West's place within the national community. Although we do not subscribe completely to Arthur Kemp's famous dictum that "demography is destiny," we do believe that numbers count, and that economic and political analysis needs to be firmly grounded in demographic realities. Many of the demographic changes that are rewriting the political script for western Canada may not be dramatic over the short run, but they have an inexorable transformative character that cannot be ignored.

Chapter 3 provides a basic overview of the regional economy, how that economy has changed over time, and how the place of western Canada within the national economy has been transformed. At the heart of the chapter lies a central question for not only western Canada but also Canada: how do we position a resource-based regional economy within the dynamics of global economic change? Is there a better future than being more technologically savvy "hewers of wood and drawers of water"? If resource extraction is our past, what is our future? The tone of this chapter is one of cautious optimism, recognizing that the regional economy has both great strengths and great challenges as we move forward.

Chapter 4 tackles the highly contested topic of regional integration, the extent to which western Canada can be seen as a regional community rather than as a shorthand statistical aggregation of four quite distinct and idiosyncratic provinces bound together only by their geographic position on the western side of the country. This topic is examined from the perspectives of both intergovernmental relations—do the four provincial governments act in concert to give institutional expression to western Canada—and citizen identifications—do western Canadians see themselves as part of a regional community?

In chapter 5 we move the focus of discussion from the West's position within Canada, within the national economy and political system, to the West's changing position within a rapidly evolving global economy. The primary concern lies with the region's ongoing economic relationship with the United States and its potential relationship with rapidly growing Asian economies. The underlying argument is that the West's position within the global economy will both determine, and be determined by, the region's place within Canada.

Chapter 6 pulls these many threads together in a discussion of how the transformation of western Canada is driving the transformation of Canada. Our thesis, to which we will return frequently, is that the economic and political transformation of the West is not a blip but instead reflects enduring structural changes in the nature of the Canadian economy and polity. Simply put, we will argue that the story of the West in Canada is becoming the story of Canada.

Throughout this analysis we are unabashed Canadian nationalists who believe that even at its peak, western discontent was a frustrated sense of Canadian nationalism. The political impulse in the West has been for greater engagement in rather than withdrawal from the national community, a determination by western Canadians to shape Canada in their own image, to create a national community that more fully reflects their values and aspirations. Although for most of the twentieth century this Don Quixote quest resulted in frustration rather than success, the early twenty-first century looks more promising. Here it is important to stress, however, that regional discontent in whatever form should not overshadow a greater reality: Canada has worked pretty well at providing its citizens with a high level of economic well-being, personal security, and civility, and western Canadians have benefited as much if not more than other Canadians. Therefore the fundamental western complaint is not that we have failed as a country, but that we could do, should do much better.

1.   The West Outside In

IN THE 1972 general election the federal Liberals were reduced to a minority government, in large part due to the drubbing the party received at the hands of the western Canadian electorate. As a response to the surge in what became known as *western alienation,* and to demonstrate the government's sensitivity to western concerns, Prime Minister Pierre Elliott Trudeau convened the 1973 Western Economic Opportunities Conference (WEOC) in Calgary. To the surprise of the federal government representatives, the western premiers presented a united front despite their marked partisan and ideological differences— three of the premiers were New Democrats, and the fourth, Peter Lougheed, was a Progressive Conservative. The premiers dominated the meeting and, from the perspective of the federal government, WEOC could only be considered a failure in demonstrating Ottawa's leadership. Former Alberta premier Don Getty, who was then a minister in Lougheed's Alberta delegation, recalls Trudeau's reaction: "At the end of the second day, I can still see him reaching forward with the gavel and hitting the wooden block and saying, 'And so ends the first and only and last Western Opportunities Conference,' and then he just let the gavel fall" (Harrington 2000). WEOC was dead, but the genie of western discontent was out of the bottle for good.

Trudeau, admittedly, was neither the first nor the last Liberal prime minister, or for that matter prime minister of any partisan stripe, to struggle with western Canada, even if his relationship was arguably the most colourful. Trudeau gained regional infamy for "giving the finger" to protesters in Salmon Arm, British Columbia, and was responsible for the extremely unpopular 1980 National Energy Program (NEP), which was seen by many western Canadians as destructive economic policy. More generally, Trudeau's rocky relationship with the West brought into sharp focus the potent combination of economic conflict and fundamentally incompatible national visions articulated in Ottawa and the West. This combination has shaped western Canadian discontent from the late 1800s to recent times.

The long story arc of regional discontent, reaching back to the early days of European settlement in western Canada, is not itself exceptional. It brings to mind the Quebec licence plate slogan, "Je me souviens," a thinly veiled or naked reference to the conquest of Quebec in 1759, or for that matter the nostalgia for independence in Newfoundland and Labrador, or the 2012 national celebration of the bicentennial of the War of 1812. In the best of Canadian political tradition, western Canadians often refer back to historical events and grievances even if their specific meaning has all but evaporated with the passage of time. (Just ask a western Canadian under the age of 60 about the Crow Rate, or freight rates in general.) There is an established historical narrative anchored by stories of protest and conflict, and told by self-described outsiders seeking a larger voice in national affairs. Although western dissatisfaction with the federal government has waxed and waned over time, it is too deeply embedded within the regional political culture—it almost *is* the regional political culture—to be easily displaced by short-term changes in economic or partisan fortunes.

Now for some readers, the notion that the West's contemporary political culture reflects distant or even very distant policy decisions and historical conflicts can be difficult to accept. They may well ask, "What does the National Policy of 1879, or for that matter the National Energy Program of 1980, have to do with my life today, in a very different West and a very different world?" Take a reader who was 21 when this book was first published, and imagine her at a coffee shop in Vancouver's West End, or having a beer at the Forks in Winnipeg:

- for all her teenage and young adult life (2006–2014), the Conservative Party with strong western representation and a Calgary-based prime minister formed the federal government;
- when the Reform Party of Canada had its electoral breakthrough in 1993, she had just been born;
- when the NEP was introduced in 1980, her *parents* were likely teenagers; and
- when the National Policy was introduced in 1879, her *great, great, great grandparents* would have been starting their families.

In our defence of the historical material to come in this chapter we would note that similar references to the Conquest of 1759 and the Plains of Abraham would not seem odd in Quebec, nor would references to the Civil War seem odd in the contemporary American South. It is not unusual in political life to have overarching themes that stretch across a multi-generational canvas, ones that in this case link the 1879 National Policy, freight rates, the NEP, and the policy challenges facing today's urban West. Moreover, and as Canadian historian Donald Creighton so wonderfully explains, "The waves behind the vessel which is carrying humanity forward into the unknown . . . can teach us where the winds of change are blowing and on what course the chief currents of our age are set. They can reveal to us the main direction of our voyage through time" (1980, 19).

In this context, however, it may be surprising that our story arc for regional discontent does not reach back to the generations of Aboriginal occupancy before European settlement, or even to the early days of the fur trade when the nascent regional economy relied so heavily on Aboriginal collaboration and skills; it begins only with the European settlement of western Canada, and more specifically with the agrarian settlement of the prairie provinces.[1] With post-Confederation agrarian settlement came a dramatic shift from economic codependence with Aboriginal peoples in the fur trade to an overwhelming interest in Aboriginal *lands,* and at best a passing interest in the welfare of the inhabitants of those lands. The pressing political issue of the day was how to open up Aboriginal lands for European settlement. Moreover, the political discontent that began to ferment within the new settlements was cast almost entirely within the institutional framework put into place by Confederation; while Aboriginal *land* was of foundational importance to the expansion of Canada, Aboriginal *peoples* at the time were seen more as a hindrance than a building block.

Admittedly, there have been attempts over the years to portray the 1875 Red River Rebellion led by Louis Riel as *the* symbol of western Canadian discontent. However, European settlers would have seen very little connection between their own grievances and those of Aboriginal peoples. The interests that Riel articulated and those of European settlers were far more conflicted than we often recognize today; Riel's portrayal as a *regional* figure reflects contemporary sensibilities that fail to capture the core of his grievances. Indeed, we would argue that casting Riel as a regional figure diminishes his very complex historical contribution. More generally, weaving Aboriginal issues and discontent into the historical warp and woof of regional discontent would distort rather than enrich our understanding of both; certainly Aboriginal issues should be addressed on their own, and not as a subset of regional discontent. Somewhat ironically, Aboriginal peoples play a limited role in the history of regional discontent but, as we will see throughout the book, they play a *much* greater role in today's efforts to secure prosperity in a rapidly changing national and global economy. If Aboriginal peoples appear to be neglected when looking back, this is by no means the case when looking forward.

Finally, the many images and examples of regional conflict brought into play by its long story arc can often obscure the more constructive, positive side of the regional voice. The political and institutional critique that western Canadians developed to explain negative economic policy also offered a set of institutional reforms through which this critique could be addressed. Rippling throughout was an emergent *national* vision that often ran counter to visions of Canada rooted in the central Canadian historical tradition. The conflict, therefore, was more than economic or regional; it was not only about the place of the West in Canada, but also about the very nature of Canada.

Economic Roots of Regional Discontent

The West was forged as a national project through policies designed to expand Canada westward from Ontario, to settle a vast territory, and to keep that territory within the British Empire. At the time of Confederation in 1867 there were no western Canadian provinces, only the Northwest Territories populated by little more than a sprinkling of European settlers and fur traders, and the small west coast colony of British Columbia. Although the Aboriginal population was significant, it was the land they occupied rather than Aboriginal peoples themselves that shaped the early visions of agrarian settlement. Here readers should be aware of the following realities:

- Confederation was spurred in part by the need to create a central government with sufficient wherewithal to drive westward expansion, and to beat the Americans to the "empty centre." This characterization of the West as open and unsettled before European immigration is not widely accepted today, particularly by Aboriginal peoples, but it was the predominant worldview at the time of European settlement.
- Confederation placed legislative responsibilities for "Indians and lands reserved for Indians" with the federal government, which therefore had the responsibility for establishing treaties with First Nations through which the West could be opened for European settlement.
- Although the federal system established in 1867 lodged responsibilities for immigration concurrently with the provincial and federal

governments, the latter was overwhelmingly the dominant player in promoting immigration abroad and creating the land entitlements for immigrants that made Canada competitive with the warmer United States.

- Law and order on the new frontier—"Peace, Order and Good Government" in the constitutional language of the day—was established by the Royal Canadian Mounted Police and codified in a national criminal code.
- The federal government was an active player in the promotion and financing of the Canadian Pacific Railroad, without which western settlers would not have had access to continental and foreign markets, and the colonists in British Columbia would not have been lured into Confederation. (British Columbia joined Confederation as a province in 1871.)
- Ottawa was the primary regulator of the new railroad and its competitors to come, and the all-important rail freight rates were established by the Canadian Parliament.
- The tariffs embedded in the 1879 National Policy (discussed in greater detail below) gave the federal government the financial means to support western expansion, including the building of a transcontinental rail system north of the 49th parallel.

All of the above formed a loosely integrated set of national policies and constitutional principles designed to open up the prairies for agricultural settlement. The West didn't just happen; it was created by an act of political will. It also came about through the massive infusion of financial capital and migrants—teachers, farmers, lawyers, retailers, ministers and entrepreneurs—from Ontario and the Maritimes. (There was very little in-migration from francophone Quebec.) Mortgages, financing for farm equipment, religious institutions, civil engineers, and educators came from afar to help settle the prairie West. It is an intriguing paradox, therefore, that the national policies that opened the door for western settlement, and to some degree the central Canadian banks that financed settlement, became the very policies and institutions around which the canon of regional discontent was built.

Part of the problem centred on perceptions of fairness. Arthur Lower's history of Canada, *From Colony to Nation* (1946), traces the country's slow and peaceful evolution from British colony to an independent country spanning the top end of North America. Within this national story is embedded the story of the West's slower emergence as an equal partner in Canada. Western Canada was a debtor region with the debt largely held by central Canadian financial institutions, and western Canadians confronted a national government that was geographically and psychologically distant from their own region and lives. The provincial ownership of natural resources, a constitutional entitlement bestowed on the founding provinces at the time of Confederation, was not realized for the prairie provinces until the 1930 *Natural Resources Transfer Act*. It is not surprising, therefore, that early perspectives on the West bordered on colonialism, as foreshadowed by an editorial that appeared in the Toronto *Globe* on March 6, 1862:

> When the territory [the West] belongs to Canada, when its navigable waters are traversed for a few years by vessels, and lines of travel are permanently established, when settlements are formed in favourable locations throughout the territory, it will not be difficult by grants of land to secure the construction of a railway across the plains and through the mountains. . . . If we set about the work of opening the territory at once, we will win the race [against the United States]. . . . It is an empire we have in view, and its whole export and import trade will be concentrated in the hands of Canadian merchants and manufacturers if we strike for it now. (Quoted in Underhill 1950, 55)

Donald Smiley, one of Canada's foremost political scientists, echoed this sentiment more than 100 years later when he wrote: "Western Canada was from the first, and to a considerable extent remains, an economic colony of the country's central heartland" (1976, 193).

Western Canadian frustration with national economic policy found early and deep roots in 1879 when Sir John A. Macdonald's Conservative government brought in the National Policy, which remained the mainstay of Canadian macro-economic policy until after World War II. The import tariffs that it imposed were designed to shield Canadian manufacturers from foreign—primarily American—competition and to encourage foreign firms to establish branch plants in Canada behind the protection of the tariff wall. In the era before personal income taxes, tariffs also generated a substantial part of the federal government's tax revenues, revenues that helped finance a national rail system linking the West to central Canadian and foreign markets. Tariffs, however, could not be used to open up international markets for Canadian crops, softwood lumber, or other natural resources. As a consequence, western farmers and natural resource producers more generally competed without tariff protection on international markets while paying the additional input costs that tariff protection imposed. This placed prairie farmers at a particular competitive disadvantage with American farmers just south of the border.

The costs of the National Policy—higher prices for imported goods—were borne by Canadians no matter where they lived, whereas the benefits—employment in the embryonic manufacturing sector—were regionally concentrated in the urban centres of Ontario and Quebec. The Policy did not mandate the location of manufacturing activities in central Canada; such decisions were driven primarily by the size of the domestic market and proximity to international markets, neither of which worked to the West's advantage. As a result, central Canada was the clear beneficiary while in the prairie West, regional costs were not offset by regional benefits. As supporters of the prairie-based Progressive Party argued in the early 1920s, the effect of the National Policy was "20 per cent less for everything we sell and 20 per cent more for everything we buy." Overall, although there is little question that tariff protection helped the development of domestic manufacturing industries, it left a very sour taste in the mouths of agricultural producers in the West. The adjective "national," which came to be associated with policies designed to assist manufacturing interests in central Canada at the direct expense of farmers in the West, was irrevocably damaged.

Agrarian frustration also arose from marketing systems and financial institutions. The early regional economy was overwhelmingly based on grain produced for export to distant foreign (primarily European) markets. The movement into world markets, however, was anything but smooth as western farmers confronted a host of challenges and uncertainties. Crop yields were subject to the vagaries of the erratic and frequently harsh Canadian climate, whereas market demand rested on independent climatic conditions in Europe and those countries, particularly the United States and Australia, who were competing for export markets. Western farmers were thousands of miles away from buyers overseas who could only be reached through extensive marketing and transportation systems beyond their immediate control; this resulted in a strong frustration with the central Canadian "middlemen" who controlled those systems and, in the eyes of western farmers, often reaped excessive profits at the expense of farmers. Agricultural settlement was dependent on securing financial credit, and the debt was held by central Canadian financial institutions that were neither knowledgeable about nor sympathetic toward the highly variable conditions confronting western farmers. There was, then, a chronic dependency on forces beyond the control of those in the region—a dependency that clashed with the fierce spirit of self-reliance animating those who wrestled a living from the prairie soil.

The "boom and bust" character of the regional economy further exacerbated the inherent problems of distance from markets and frontier debt. Good crops and strong export markets could bring handsome

rewards just as weak markets and poor crops due to early frost, grasshoppers, and/or drought could bring disaster. To paraphrase the Henry
Wadsworth Longfellow's children's poem, when times were good—
when markets were strong, the regional climate favourable, and interest
rates low—they were very, very good, and when times were bad—when
markets were weak, grasshoppers were plentiful, frosts came early, and
credit was expensive—they were horrid.

To be fair, many of the challenges faced by prairie farmers were
beyond the control of the most sympathetic federal governments. Even
with the best of will, Ottawa could not control the weather or move
the West closer to global markets, although transportation infrastructure and regulated freight rates could certainly moderate the financial
effects of distance. Nonetheless, standing between western farmers and
international markets were a host of national programs and policies
that did have an impact on regional prosperity. The federal government
set the tariffs on imported goods and thereby affected many of the input
costs for agricultural production, including the cost of farm machinery.
Ottawa set both rail freight rates and the more general regulatory framework for the railways linking the West to international markets, as well
as regulating the financial institutions upon which western Canadian
farmers were dependent. By the late 1930s, the Canadian Wheat Board
was the monopoly marketing body through which prairie grain production (but not grain produced in Ontario) had to move to reach foreign
markets. In some cases, of course, federal actions were seen as being
beneficial to regional economic interests: the introduction of the Crow
Rate in 1897, which capped the freight rates on unprocessed grain moving out of the prairies, was supported throughout most of the twentieth
century, as was the Wheat Board. Yet despite these steps, and perhaps
unfairly, the actions of the federal government were generally viewed as
exploitative rather than supportive of the West. They were seen to serve
the financial, transportation, and manufacturing interests of Montreal
and Toronto more than the interests of prairie homesteaders.

This, then, was the economic and political legacy left by the wheat
economy that so dominated the prairie economy during the early decades
of the twentieth century. It was a cosmopolitan legacy infused with radical British Labour ideas brought to the prairies by British immigrants,
and with populist ideologies brought north by American immigrants—
and by the social media of the times that included American speak-
ers and publications. Interestingly, this legacy continued to frame the
regional political narrative long after the grain economy lost its grip on
the region. As the primary motors of the prairie economy shifted more
to oil, natural gas, and petrochemicals in Alberta, to a broader resource

base in British Columbia and Saskatchewan, and to a diversified manufacturing and financial services economy in Manitoba, there was still a pervasive assumption that national policies were skewed in favour of the central Canadian provinces. This perspective was reinforced with the 1980 National Energy Program that capped the domestic Canadian price for oil well below international prices, thereby reducing returns to western Canadian producers and provincial governments, primarily Alberta. The NEP also sought to direct new energy investment onto federal Crown Lands (Canada Lands), particularly in the North, thereby limiting potential growth in provincial royalties. Had the NEP been fully implemented it would have reduced industry revenues from a barrel of oil from 45 per cent to 28 per cent, reduced provincial revenues from 45 per cent to below 36 per cent, and increased federal government revenues from 10 per cent to "at least 36%" by 1983 (Scarfe 1981, 6–8). As Scarfe wrote at the time, "Since the consumer and the federal government are the main winners in the energy program, it is obvious that the producers and the provincial governments of the producing provinces (especially Alberta) along with the residents they represent will be the losers" (1981, 8).

Together, the 1879 National Policy and the 1980 National Energy Program bracketed and exemplified more than a century of public policy in which western regional interests were sacrificed on the altar of a very narrowly defined national interest. The widely held perspective that regional interests were routinely given short shrift shaped interpretations of even relatively minor events, such as the federal government's 1986 decision to award the CF-18 aircraft maintenance contract to a Montreal firm despite a technically superior bid from a Winnipeg firm (Campbell and Pal 1989). As Pat Burns, hotline radio host for Vancouver's CJOR, argued at the time of the CF-18 decision:

> Despite the fact that the Winnipeg-based Bristol Aerospace put in a lower bid and had a track record to show they were superior, Canadair, in Montreal, ended up with the more-than-one-billion-dollar contract to service the CF-18 fighter planes Canada is buying from the United States. Quebec was superior in only one aspect. It has 75 federal seats, Manitoba 14. That and that alone is what got the contract for Canadair. (As quoted in Western Concept Party 1993, 3)

The experiences of the wheat economy, writ large in regional scope and long in time, became the past and contemporary experience of the West as a whole, with new events and grievances updating an old story. Although in some cases western Canadians exaggerated the negative impact of national policies on regional prosperity, this is beside the point. Fact is no match for mythology in framing political cultures, in the West or elsewhere.

To summarize, a comprehensive regional critique emerged in the West that tied specific policy grievances to the nature of Canadian party politics, federalism, and parliamentary institutions. This critique first developed in step with the agricultural settlement of the prairie provinces when a core set of economic grievances, lightly laced with cultural conflict (discussed below), characterized the early decades of the grain economy. These grievances led in turn to the charge that national policies exacerbated rather than moderated a host of challenges confronting the pioneer community. The critique sank deeply into the regional political culture because so many western Canadians were linked directly or indirectly to the pervasive grain economy. And, because the grievances were so widely shared, the critique was easily communicated. It then took on new dimensions as Canada moved through the latter half of the twentieth century. Rather than being discarded as a relic of the early years of the grain economy, the regional critique took on renewed vigour for western Canadians still lacking an effective voice in the national political system.

Against this backdrop, specific policy disputes assumed deeper symbolic meaning. The National Policy, freight rates, the failure to grant provincial ownership of natural resources until 1930, and the NEP all represent more than policy grievances; they were potent symbols, interpretative guides to the West's rocky relationship with the federal government and the larger Canadian community. As Laurie Blakeman, an Alberta Liberal MLA, explains: "The NEP has taken on an iconic status. . . . Most people in Alberta today don't even know what it was. They couldn't tell you what the three initials stood for. But it is representative of things that they're unhappy with—other people trying to take what they believe is theirs" (as quoted in Bennett 2012). It is through this lens of perceived economic exploitation that many western Canadians, and many western Canadian political actors, continue to view national policy debates. For example, current-day proposals to create a Canadian energy strategy, or to price carbon, are at least initially viewed by some through the lens of the NEP experience.

Before leaving our discussion of this historical backdrop it is important to acknowledge the dominance of prairie concerns in our formulation of western discontent. And, to be sure, the principal historical cauldron of political radicalism was the grain economy that knit Manitoba, Saskatchewan, and Alberta into an integrated economic region and therefore into a loosely integrated political region. The three provinces had a shared reliance on the grain economy and on the federal policies that supported or frustrated that economy. Although the three provincial economies were far from identical, their economic similarities were striking, as were the differences between the grain economy and the industrial economy that was beginning to take shape in Ontario and Quebec. In most respects, therefore, it was *agrarian discontent* that shaped the prairie political culture, and this discontent spilled over the mountains into British Columbia in only a very muted form. An exception here, but truly an exception, is the Social Credit movement that originated in the Alberta dust bowl of the 1930s, but then, shedding its agrarian colouration as it did so, expanded in the early 1950s into British Columbia under the populist leadership of W.A.C. Bennett.

Although agriculture was by no means missing from the BC economy, it took very different forms and had a much less pervasive social, economic, and, therefore, political impact. Political conflict in British Columbia was based more on regional conflict *within* the province—more on social class than on disagreements over national policies, although the latter were far from absent. Labour unions were much more active players in the BC political arena than they were on the prairies. Thus, W.L. Morton, the foremost scholar of radical agrarian politics, wrote about "the bias of prairie politics" (1970). From this perspective there have been two quite distinct western Canadas: the prairie West and British Columbia, sometimes dubbed "the West beyond the West" (Barman 1993), and it is the latter that is often overlooked in historical treatments of western Canadian politics. This neglect is only partly explained by the province's relatively light demographic heft until fairly contemporary times; British Columbia's current position as the West's demographic powerhouse, with 42.7 per cent of the regional population at the time of the 2011 census, is of relatively recent vintage. It is our argument, however, and one that the reader should hold in abeyance for now, that the "bias of prairie politics" has morphed over time into *a more general regional critique* that includes significant elements of political life on the west coast. As the focus of discontent moved from specific economic grievances emerging directly from the prairie grain economy to the underlying political critique used to explain those grievances, the language of discontent became more *regionally* inclusive.

The West's Political Critique

Over the past century western Canada gave birth to a large number and a great variety of political movements and parties expressing a wide array of grievances while offering an equally wide array of potential reforms. Some of the parties and movements, including the Progressive Party of Canada and the Reform Party of Canada, focused entirely on federal politics. Others, such as the United Farmers of Alberta, Manitoba's Nonpartisan League and, more recently, the Saskatchewan Party, have had a provincial focus. Still others, such as Social Credit and the Cooperative Commonwealth Federation (CCF), spilled across federal and provincial politics. And, some parties that campaigned and governed under national party labels were in many ways as radical in their stance to Canadian political life as those parties more readily identified as protest parties—here the BC and Saskatchewan Liberals and the Alberta Progressive Conservatives come to mind.

The challenge for authors—and for readers!—is to make sense of this rich cacophony of voices. One solution would be to present a chronological account of the evolving political landscape in western Canada, from 1867 to today, but there have been too many players spread across too much time and geography to make this approach manageable. Furthermore, while we recognize the importance of history, our primary goal in this chapter is to set the stage for a more contemporary analysis, to speculate on what the future might hold. Thus, instead of a chronological account we have decided to focus on a handful of central themes and, to paraphrase Donald Creighton, to determine to what extent they reveal the main direction of the western Canadian political voyage through time. Although we will draw upon specific parties and movements for examples and illustrations, a detailed analysis or even a description of specific players is beyond the scope of this work.

This solution, however, is far neater in theory than in practice. Identifying themes that hold up over more than a century of political discontent, and finding themes that have found expression across a very diverse political and geographic landscape is not easy. When the canvas is so large, weaving together a regional story that makes sense for the reader mentioned above, having a coffee in Vancouver's West End or a beer at the Winnipeg Forks, is inevitably contentious. Let's begin, then, by clearing away some of the underbrush, identifying some things that are *not* significant or overarching features of regional discontent in western Canada.

What Western Regional Discontent Is *Not* About

It would be a mistake to see regional discontent at any time or in any of the four provinces as *primarily* ideological discontent, and especially as a quest for smaller or more limited government. The regional culture has embraced parties and movements on the right and left, and everywhere in-between. The Progressive Party in the 1920s knit together a broad set of agrarian interests and grievances that are hard to locate in terms of left and right, and some of the parties conventionally placed on the political right embraced a very active role for governments. The Depression years of the mid-1930s saw the almost simultaneous creation of both the left-of-centre CCF, which would eventually morph into the NDP, and the ostensibly right-of-centre Social Credit; the former became a mainstay party in Saskatchewan for generations and the latter formed the provincial government in Alberta from 1935 to 1971. Even here, though, it is not at all clear that the different ideological leanings of the two parties resulted in much of a difference in style or substance. Indeed, party labels can be poor predictors of action: Alberta's Progressive Conservative governments, which have held office since 1971, have consistently led the country in terms of per capita spending, and BC's Social Credit governments were emphatic province-builders through such initiatives as BC Hydro and BC Ferries. Even the Reform Party, we would argue (and others may well disagree), was far more about the "West wants in" in its early days than it was about smaller government or a more conservative social agenda. Western discontent has been many things, but it has never been a coherent or consistent *ideological* assault on the Canadian status quo. Ideology has done more to fragment than unite the West.

In addition to not being an ideological critique, western discontent is not a cultural critique; cultural differences between the West and the rest do not drive the fundamentals of regional discontent. Western Canadians, unlike Quebecers, are unlikely to proclaim a distinctive regional culture—or for that matter distinctive provincial cultures within the region—that merits political protection beyond conventional public support for arts and culture. Few see the West as a "distinct society" or attach much political significance to the distinctive features that do exist. There is no support for nor is there interest in constitutional protection for a distinct regional culture or society; there is no interest, as there is in Quebec, in transferring power over culture and communications from Ottawa to provincial governments. While the Calgary Stampede is used both to assert and deride a unique southern Alberta culture, at the very most this is a small bit of cultural spice in the much larger stew of economically driven regional discontent. Westerners are not about to throw up barricades in the streets to protect regionally rooted or provincially rooted cultural differences.

The contrast with Quebec with respect to constitutional authority for communications and culture is important in a broader sense. Nationalists in Quebec have consistently sought a federal state in which provincial governments, and particularly the government of Quebec, would exercise greater constitutional authority and the federal government would exercise less. In the extreme, the devolution of authority to Quebec could reach the point where what is today a province would be indistinguishable from a sovereign state. By contrast, regional discontent in the West has rarely been associated with a call for greater devolution, for reducing the constitutional authority of the federal government. Instead, the call has been for greater political influence *within* the federal government and not for bringing the constitutional authority of the federal government home to the provinces. A major exception, of course, was the campaign for the 1930 *Natural Resources Transfer Act* that relinquished Ottawa's authority with respect to natural resource ownership in the West so that the prairie provinces had the same authority as other provinces. This exception, however, illustrates the more general rule: western discontent has not been about any fundamental redesign of Canadian federalism but rather about more equitable treatment *within* the federal system. The contrast with the nationalist movement in Quebec is profound; western Canadians want in, not out. Here it is important to note that although separatist movements have occasionally erupted in the West, particularly in Alberta and in the wake of the NEP, they have never commanded any significant degree of electoral support beyond the rare by-election flash in the pan.

The fact that western Canadians are unexceptional in their attitudes toward Canada and the current division of powers is demonstrated by data drawn from the 2011 Canadian Election Study (CES).[2] Western Canadians, it turns out, are remarkably similar to Atlantic and Ontario residents when it comes to positive feeling about Canada, and to the belief that their provincial governments, rather than the federal government, have the most impact on their lives (see Table 1.1). It is Quebecers who stand out with their more muted enthusiasm for Canada and their stronger preferences for the provincial government. Ontarians, on the other hand, stand alone in feeling that the federal government should have stronger powers than the provincial government.

In a similar vein, support for the Americanization of the Canadian political system should not be read into western Canadian discontent, something that was frequently done by critics of the Reform Party's advocacy of Senate reform. Admittedly, the visceral anti-Americanism that often colours Canadian nationalism in Ontario is much less present in the West where the political culture has been untouched by the legacy of the United Empire Loyalists or the War of 1812. The Canadian–American relationship on the western half of the continent has been and is much more congenial, and during the agrarian settlement of the prairie West there was an extensive exchange of ideas, publications, visionary

TABLE 1.1 Attitudes toward Federalism by Region[3]

	FEELINGS ABOUT CANADA	SHOULD HAVE STRONGER POWERS	GOVERNMENT WITH MOST IMPACT ON LIFE
Atlantic Canada	Mean = 94.9	Federal—41.9% Provincial—45.8%	Federal—28.5% Provincial—49.7%
Quebec	Mean = 78.6	Federal—28.1% Provincial—65.0%	Federal—16.9% Provincial—55.1%
Ontario	Mean = 92.4	Federal—54.5% Provincial—31.6%	Federal—28.2% Provincial—45.4%
Western Canada	Mean = 93.2	Federal—44.6% Provincial—41.5%	Federal—26.7% Provincial—45.4%
NATIONAL	Mean = 89.1	Federal—42.6% Provincial—45.7%	Federal—25.1% Provincial—46.1%

SOURCE: Canada Election Study 2011, as derived by authors. Data are weighted.

leadership, and settlers. In British Columbia, relationships along the west coast from San Francisco to Alaska tended to be as important as the more distant relationships with the rest of Canada. While it would be an overstatement to argue that anti-Americanism is absent west of the Lake of the Woods, it is much less virulent and much less deeply engrained in the political culture. Moreover, it has not translated into support for the Americanization of Canadian politics or institutions; there are ample domestic reasons to support Senate reform (or, for that matter, abolition)! The border was there, but it did not shape the region or emerging regional conceptions of Canadian nationalism.

Finally, it is important not to associate western discontent with a particular provincial epicenter within the region. Although Alberta has "led the charge" since the OPEC-induced spike in oil prices during the 1970s, and although Alberta's political leaders have been prone to speak for the West on the national stage, to conflate provincial and regional interests, the West's political centre has been far more fluid than recent experience would suggest. In the early decades of the twentieth century, Winnipeg was unquestionably the regional heartland—it was the West's only true urban centre, the locus of financial institutions, the region's transportation and marketing hub, and the source of many of the most creative political ideas. Saskatchewan's CCF governments in the 1950s, unlike Social Credit governments in Alberta, blazed new social policy trails that have had a lasting national impact. In the decades to come, British Columbia may well displace Alberta's regional leadership as the interaction of resource development, a strong environmental movement, and the gravitational pull of Asia play out within the West's largest province. And, overlying the region as a whole will be a set of Aboriginal challenges and opportunities that have no specific provincial home, although here again British Columbia will be front and centre. Thus, if asked, "When you say 'the West' do you really mean 'Alberta'?" the answer is an emphatic no.

What Western Regional Discontent Is About: The Core Critique

Enough, then, about what western discontent is *not*. Apart from the specific economic grievances discussed earlier, what have been the major themes expressed within the western Canadian political critique— themes that have set the region apart from the rest of Canada while at the same time pulling together seemingly disparate western provinces? The following closely entangled themes capture a large portion although by no means the entirety of western Canada's political critique. Readers should note at the outset, however, that these themes were not always present, and some were more pronounced at specific times and places. It would be a mistake to assume, for example, that the United Farmers of Alberta, the Saskatchewan CCF, and the Reform Party all sang from the same hymnbook, or to assume that the quest for Senate reform has been an enduring or ubiquitous quest in the West. It should also be noted that we have committed some conceptual violence in disentangling themes that were part of a more tightly interwoven story than our compartmentalization might suggest. Although western discontent can best be seen as a rich tapestry, unfortunately, we have little option but to pull on some of the individual threads.

Frustration with the Conventions of Parliamentary Government

Through long and bitter experience, western Canadians became convinced that the conventions of parliamentary government choked off an effective regional voice, and as a consequence national economic policies too often failed to reflect western interests and aspirations adequately. Western Canadian MPs, of course, were quite appropriately a minority in the House, just as western Canadians were a minority in the national population, but even a minority voice was rendered more difficult when parliamentary conventions dictated that decisions were best taken in secret, behind the closed doors of caucus and cabinet. Thus, a fundamental tenet of open government, that justice is not only done but seen to be done, was violated. To the extent that western MPs and cabinet

ministers had influence, and they often did, it was exercised aw
the eyes and ears of their constituents. Cabinet secrecy and ﹖
were especially problematic; when a cabinet decision went aga﹍
region it was impossible for voters to tell if their cabinet representatives had fought the good fight but lost, had traded a loss today for a
win tomorrow, or had simply rolled over in the face of pressure from
their numerically dominant central Canadian counterparts in cabinet.
Parliamentary conventions preclude open government, and it was open
government that many western Canadians sought.

Parliamentary conventions understandably rankle most with parts of
the electorate that end up on the losing side in general elections, and
western Canadians have displayed an almost uncanny ability to pick the
losing side. Until recently, western Canadians have typically found their
MPs sitting on the opposition benches; between 1965 and 2000, less
than one-third of western Canadian MPs were in the governing party
(Roach 2003, 4). For the most part, western Canadian MPs and their
constituents were outsiders looking in, and from that vantage point parliamentary government left a lot to be desired. True, the western provinces were strongly represented in Progressive Conservative governing
caucuses, with three-quarters of western seats in 1979 and 1984, and
one-half of western seats in 1988 being on the government side of the
House. However, Progressive Conservative governments were the exception in the twentieth century and the Liberal party, Canada's 'natural
governing party,' had far less robust western representation. In six of the
seven Liberal governments between 1965 and the turn of the century,
less than 20 per cent of western Canadian seats were on the government side of the House (Roach 2003, 4). But this reality was precisely
what aggravated western Canadians; why should an effective voice in
the national Parliament be dependent on electoral support for a single
party? Surely basic fairness demanded something better?

Populism

The flip side of frustration with the conventions of parliamentary government has been a broad and deep streak of populism that weaves
its way throughout western Canadian discontent. Although this was
formally expressed in the Reform Party's assertion of "the common
sense of the common people," the sentiment has by no means been
restricted to Reform. While Canada in the past was described as a
"deferential society," elite deference in the West was tempered by the
fact that most elites—political, cultural, economic, media—came from
outside the region and, in a sweeping generalization, seldom stooped

to addressing regional concerns and aspirations. At the time of agrarian settlement there was unquestionably a city mouse/country mouse divide between the cosmopolitan centre and the rural West, one that is still reflected in the contemporary culture. It was Glen Gould versus Ian Tyson; CBC versus talk radio hosts such as Dave Rutherford in Calgary, John Gormley in Saskatoon, and Bill Good in Vancouver; Leonard Cohen versus Neil Young; Margaret Atwood versus W.P. Kinsella. Perhaps the most pronounced political expression of western populism came with the Reform Party's demand that the 1992 Charlottetown constitutional accord be submitted to the Canadian people in a referendum and not left for ratification by the federal, provincial, and territorial legislatures. The Reform Party prevailed, and the accord went down to a stunning defeat despite endorsement—sometimes half-hearted—by the governments of the day. Whether this was a good outcome for the country is still hotly debated by constitutional elites, but within the West it has been widely accepted as a victory for "the common sense of the common people."

It should be noted that the western Canadian reform impulse with respect to parliamentary government in Ottawa, the desire to loosen the bounds of party discipline and cabinet secrecy, did not spill over into a similar quest for *provincial* institutional reform. True, western Canadians have dabbled with electoral reform: British Columbia brought in a new electoral system in 1951 and, in its wake, a new Social Credit government that promptly went back to the old system; BC residents defeated electoral reform referenda in 2005 (very narrowly) and 2009 (less narrowly); Alberta uses Senatorial "selections" to provide advice to the Prime Minister on Senate appointment; and the western provinces have led the national adoption of fixed election dates. Further, Alberta's *Taxpayer Protection Act* requires referendum consent before new taxes can be implemented, BC voters ousted the Harmonized Sales Tax through a provincial referendum, and in the 1930s and early 1940s, Manitoba experimented with a nominally nonpartisan legislative assembly. In total, however, western Canada has not been a cauldron of democratic reform when it comes to the conduct of provincial legislative politics. Alberta, the province that has led so much of the regional charge for parliamentary reform in Ottawa, has been particularly steadfast in its commitment to the institutional status quo within the province.

As in the case of frustration with the conventions of parliamentary government, the West's populist streak is much more apparent when it comes to federal politics than it is in the operation and style of provincial governments. Populism is certainly present in the provincial arenas, but not necessarily more so than in other regions of the country. It is a key component of the *federal* political culture in the West while finding more limited expression in provincial politics.

Fairness and Equality

In many ways the bottom line for western Canadian discontent is a conviction that the national political system is unfair, that it is skewed in many ways big and small to the advantage of other regions, most notably Ontario and Quebec. (The position of Atlantic Canada in the national political system, and the potential for common cause, have never figured prominently among western Canadians who rail about the neglect of the West while at the same time rarely thinking of Canada in terms that reach east beyond Quebec City.) Perceptions of unfairness can be difficult to document or address in any empirical sense, for they are just that, perceptions. The political fact remains, however, that many western Canadians are convinced they are playing with a stacked deck and a biased if not necessarily crooked dealer. Here a critically important contributor to the sense of grievance to come was the federal government's decision in 1905 to create two new provinces—Alberta and Saskatchewan—rather than a single province due to concerns that such a province, with the flood of immigration into the prairies, could well challenge the hegemony of Ontario and Quebec.

The regional quest for greater fairness found its most concrete expression in the demand for the constitutional equality of the provinces. This demand was successfully captured in the 1930 *Natural Resources Transfer Act* that put the prairie provinces on the same constitutional footing with respect to resource ownership as the other provinces (Janigan 2012). It was also captured in the 1982 constitutional amending formulae that placed all provinces on an equal footing, providing none with a veto unavailable to others. More recently, it has been expressed in the proposed Triple E model for Senate reform whereby a reformed Senate would be elected, effective and *equal,* with all provinces having the same number of seats. (The current distribution of Senate seats is highly unequal: Quebec and Ontario each have 24 Senators; New Brunswick and Nova Scotia each have 10; British Columbia, Alberta, Saskatchewan, Manitoba, and Newfoundland and Labrador each have six; PEI has four; and the territories each have one.) Here we must note that the push for Senate reform has been a relatively late entry into the institutional reform sweepstakes. Although the Senate was never a popular institution in western Canada, or anywhere for that matter, a concerted movement for reform did not emerge until the early 1980s, led by the Committee for a Triple E Senate (backstopped by the Canada

West Foundation) and then championed by the Reform Party from its conception in 1986, and by the Government of Alberta. Canada had a brief flirtation with Senate reform during the constitutional dance around the Meech Lake Accord in the late 1980s and the Charlottetown Accord in the early 1990s, but the notion failed to gain any significant political traction outside the West until the election of the Conservative government in 2006.

Since then, the Harper government has advanced a reform agenda that includes term limits and a commitment to appoint Senators selected through provincial elections, as has been the case for the last five Senate appointments from Alberta. The government's proposals did not elicit a great deal of public support and only erratic governmental support—BC Premier Christy Clark, Saskatchewan Premier Brad Wall, and Manitoba Premier Greg Salinger all expressed modest support—but the proposals did succeed in fanning the flames of the Senate reform debate, including a renewed interest in abolition. Then, in early 2013, the reform agenda temporarily ground to a halt when the federal government asked the Supreme Court in a reference case whether it has the constitutional authority to proceed without provincial consent. (The Court's decision will likely come in 2015.) Whether the Senate expense scandals that erupted in the spring of 2013 will put new wind into the reform sails or promote greater support for abolition remains to be seen, although it is interesting that Premier Wall's tepid support for reform has been transformed into much more aggressive support for abolition.

It should also be stressed that the federal government's agenda to date does not address provincial equality within a reformed Senate, an initiative that would almost certainly require constitutional amendment and provincial consent. Here two points must be made about the regional quest for provincial equality in the Senate. First, this quest runs up against the determination of Quebecers to secure constitutional recognition of Quebec's distinct or special status within the Canadian federal state, to ensure that Quebec is neither seen nor treated as a province like the others. These conflicting constitutional visions bring to the fore how the western Canadian political critique is thoroughly entangled with regional perspectives on Quebec's place within the federation (to be discussed shortly). Second, were the Triple E model to be implemented it would do little to capture the growing demographic strength of the West. True, the region's share of Senate seats would increase from approximately 23 per cent today to approximately 39 per cent (depending on the representation of the three territories and, potentially, Aboriginal peoples). At the same time, the proportionate weight of Alberta and British Columbia in the Senate would be *less* than their proportionate weight in the House of Commons. The winners, if that is the right word, would be Manitoba, Saskatchewan, and Atlantic Canada; the four Atlantic provinces, with only with 7 per cent of the national population, could end up with close to 40 per cent of the Senate seats. This would be even more skewed than the current situation where the Atlantic provinces have almost 29 per cent of the Senate seats. It is perhaps not surprising, therefore, that the goal of true "rep by pop" in the House—equality of citizens rather than equality of provinces—is starting to receive as much attention as Senate reform in British Columbia and Alberta. What is more surprising is that the Atlantic provinces are not more enthusiastic champions of Senate reform.

Resentment about Quebec

It is impossible to discuss western perceptions of an unfair political system without coming to grips with perceptions of Quebec within the region. Western frustration about the lack of influence in Parliament has been compounded by the perception that the even smaller Quebec tail—approximately 24 per cent of the national population—has had far greater success in wagging the Canadian dog. Until recently, the most compelling evidence for the lack of fairness came from Quebec's domination of national political leadership. In the 38 years from 1968 and the first election of Pierre Trudeau's Liberal government to the 2006 election of Stephen Harper's minority Conservative government, the prime minister of Canada came from Quebec for 36 years, with the handful of western Canadian prime ministers—Joe Clark for 9 months in 1979–80, John Turner for a few months in 1984, and Kim Campbell for an equally brief period in 1993—being no more than trivial exceptions to Quebec's dominance. (During this period no prime minister came from Ontario or Atlantic Canada, a fact that provided little solace for western Canadians.) Given this dominance, western Canadians were often mystified by the desire of many Quebecers for a more devolved federation, or even to leave the country altogether, when Quebec seemed to control most levers of power in the Canadian government.

Bilingualism has been a related flashpoint in the relationship between Quebec and the West, one that goes back to the early days of agrarian settlement. Depictions of Canada as a bilingual society never reflected the frontier experience in western Canada where francophones from Quebec were greatly outnumbered by immigrants from other linguistic backgrounds. The great social project on the prairies was to assimilate a polyglot society through a common language, English, and in this context the protection of the French language was seen as an unwelcome shield behind which other and, on the prairies, much larger ethnic groups could seek similar protection from assimilation. The primary means toward this end, as was the case in the United States, was a strong, *unilingual* public education system where a common English language provided the social and cultural glue—a melting pot more than a mosaic. The concern was not with ethnic diversity per se, for such diversity was a defining characteristic of a region built by waves of immigration from a great variety of source countries. The concern was with the public space, with an integrating language of politics, public service, and commerce. Canada might be bilingual, but the West was not, although in this case as in so many others, Manitoba more closely approximated the national norm than did the three provinces farther to the west. Even in Manitoba, however, constitutional protections for the French language were at best honoured more in word than in deed.

When the 1965 report of the Royal Commission on Bilingualism and Biculturalism called for the formal constitutional recognition of Canada as a bilingual and bicultural country, western Canadians pushed back, unsuccessfully in the case of bilingualism, but successfully in the case of biculturalism. The notion that Canada should be seen as a bi-national community was a hard sell in the West well before the political awakening of First Nations made this language particularly problematic. Official bilingualism was seen as a barrier to an effective regional voice within the national government, and as a barrier, although not an insurmountable barrier, to western Canadians considering a career in the federal public service or its supporting national associations.

The complexities of the western Canadian approach to melting pots in the public sphere and mosaics in the private sphere can be nicely illustrated by the impact of John George Diefenbaker, prime minister of Canada from 1957 to 1963. In many ways Diefenbaker was the archetypical prairie radical, a populist who drew directly from the region's pioneer experience. He was a "windmill tilter" without equal and a vociferous opponent of official bilingualism. He was an unrepentant anglophile and a symbol of the rapidly vanishing rural, small-town West. However, and it is a big however, he also won the largest landslide in Canadian federal politics when his Progressive Conservative party swept to a majority government in 1958, winning 208 of 265 seats.[4] His win led western Canada into the Progressive Conservative camp where it stayed until his party was slowly absorbed by the Reform Party, the Canadian Alliance, and finally the Conservative Party of Canada.[5] In our context, the striking thing is that the West captured the Progressive Conservative party as much as the party captured the allegiance of western Canadian voters. From Diefenbaker forward, *national* parties became the primary vehicles for regional discontent, including the short-lived Reform Party *of Canada*.

Diefenbaker, too readily dismissed as an anomaly in a long period of federal Liberal rule, also left another indelible mark on Canada. In 1960 his government introduced and Parliament proclaimed the Canadian Bill of Rights, the generally unacknowledged precursor to the 1982 Charter of Rights and Freedoms.[6] Although Pierre Trudeau can legitimately be seen as the father of the Charter, he built on Diefenbaker's initiative. The importance of this linkage is that in many ways both the Bill and the Charter reflected a commitment to individual equality that had deep roots in the western frontier (or at least the prairie frontier). In this context, Denis Smith speaks of Diefenbaker as follows:

> He gave to the Prairies for the first time in their history the same sense of dynamic and central participation in nation-building that his predecessor, John A. Macdonald, had given to central Canada after 1867 . . . [his policies] *were policies of national integration that typify the prairie conception of Canada.* (1970, 41; emphasis added)

Unfortunately, but perhaps inevitably, that prairie conception of Canada did not provide space for the new Quebec that emerged from the Quiet Revolution of the 1960s. In this sense, Diefenbaker's timing could not have been worse as the country rushed to accommodate the growing nationalist movement in Quebec and thus ward off the threat of separatism.

In summary, and contrary to the constitutional evolution discussed below, the perception that when push comes to shove Quebec wins and the West loses, that national politics is too often a losing zero-sum conflict for western Canadians, is deeply embedded within the regional culture. The 2011 Canadian Election Study data demonstrate that, compared to residents of other regions, western Canadians feel less positively about Quebec,[7] are more likely to feel that the federal government should "do less" for Quebec, and are less supportive of official bilingualism (see Table 1.2).

An online poll of 1,795 English-language speaking respondents living outside Quebec, conducted by Abacus Research in the summer of 2012, suggests that western Canadians are not alone in their ambivalence

TABLE 1.2 Attitudes toward Canada, Quebec, and Bilingualism[8]

	FEELINGS ABOUT QUEBEC	"DO LESS" FOR QUEBEC	TOO FAR PUSHING BILINGUALISM
Atlantic Canada	Mean = 68.0	Somewhat—19.5% Much—8.3% Total less—27.8%	Strongly—13.3% Somewhat—29.3% Total agree—42.6%
Quebec	Mean = 80.1	Somewhat—1.4% Much—1.1% Total less—2.5%	Strongly—4.1% Somewhat—12.0% Total agree—16.1%
Ontario	Mean = 67.9	Somewhat—16.8% Much—11.6% Total less —28.4%	Strongly—18.8% Somewhat—31.3% Total agree—50.1%
Western Canada	Mean = 62.7	Somewhat—20.7% Much—18.6% Total less—39.3%	Strongly—24.8% Somewhat—35.2% Total agree—60.0%
NATIONAL	Mean = 70.1	Somewhat—13.9% Much—10.1% Total less—24.0%	Strongly—16.2% Somewhat—27.5% Total agree—43.7%

SOURCE: Canada Election Study 2011, as derived by authors. Data are weighted.

toward Quebec (Akin 2012). Across the board there was very little support for any concessions to placate Quebec; only 12 per cent of the survey respondents agreed that "the federal government should do all it can to keep Quebec part of Canada, even if it requires special treatment." When asked how they would vote if all Canadians could vote in a referendum on the future of Quebec in Confederation, only 52 per cent of respondents reported that they would vote to keep Quebec in Canada while 26 per cent stated that they would vote to remove Quebec (22 per cent were unsure how they would vote). Among western Canadian respondents, 26 per cent of those in British Columbia would vote to remove Quebec, as would 29 per cent of those in Manitoba/ Saskatchewan, and 36 per cent of those in Alberta.

It is difficult to tell what lies ahead in the complex and often rocky relationship between Quebec and the West. It could well be that as Quebec's demographic and economic weight continues to erode, Quebec and the old national unity agenda will slowly fade from the screen in western Canada, that resentment will give way to indifference. In the emerging Canada, Diefenbaker's vision may turn out to have greater traction than his detractors could ever have imagined. However, with the federal New Democrats and Liberals both led by Quebec leaders, with Quebec likely to be a key battleground in the 2015 federal election, with a PQ government in Quebec and Alberta Premier Alison Redford winning national credibility through her fluency in both official languages, the national unity politics of tomorrow may not be that different from those of yesterday. In the words of Yogi Berra, it may be "like déjà vu all over again."

Aversion to Partisanship

A major part of the western critique of parliamentary government has been that MPs are forced by the conventions of party discipline to put the interests of their political party ahead of the interests of their province or region. This constraint on representation would have been of less concern had the parties been regionally balanced, and had the majority of MPs not represented central Canadian constituencies. Given that neither was the case, western Canadians looked for opportunities to weaken the constraints of party discipline and frequently supported alternatives to the mainstream parties. In some cases, protest parties were committed to nonpartisanship in the House of Commons; in 1921, for example, the Progressive Party won enough seats to form the official opposition in the House but declined to do so, arguing they would then be forced to operate as a disciplined party rather than as a loose coalition of radical reformers.

The bottom line here is somewhat difficult to determine. Although the western electorate frequently expressed frustration with what was seen as excessive partisanship within the mainstream parties and their behaviour in the House of Commons, this frustration often gave birth to new parties rather than a principled (and unrealistic) commitment to nonpartisanship. Many provincial parties in the West rejected any formal affiliation with their federal counterparts—note the Liberal Party of British Columbia and the Progressive Conservative Party of Alberta—but they were parties nevertheless. Provincial efforts at legislative nonpartisanship, most notably the Nonpartisan League in Manitoba, had at best limited lasting impact on their province or region, although Wesley (2011) argues that "transpartisanship" is a recessive strain of Manitoba's political culture. Certainly there is nothing in the four western provinces today that comes even close to the full-blown nonpartisanship now characteristic of the legislative assemblies of the Northwest and Nunavut Territories.

In Summary

The history of western Canadian discontent rotated around the desire for the reform of parliamentary institutions, including the political parties that populated those institutions, and ultimately around the need for national economic policies that more adequately reflected regional interests and aspirations. At the same time, western Canadians and their political leaders were more than whiners and malcontents; they were also visionaries, articulating an alternative national vision based on regional equity, economic growth, democratic ideals, and a passion for engaging the world. Although often expressed through protest politics, this western vision was an alternate nation-building perspective that has struggled to gain a national audience. Regional discontent can thus be seen as *a frustrated sense of Canadian nationalism,* and the reform impulse has always been for greater inclusion rather than withdrawal, a determination by western Canadians to shape Canada in their own image, to create a national community that more fully reflects regional values and aspirations. It is no wonder that the founding slogan of the Reform Party—"The West Wants In!"—resonated so well within the region.

Future of Western Discontent

In this chapter, we have traced the historical roots of western discontent and have noted the core dimensions of the western critique of Canadian national politics. But what is the current state of western discontent? One might expect it to be in decline; after all, most western Canadian MPs now sit on the government side of the House (although still constituting a minority in cabinet), the Harper Conservatives are making efforts to substantively reform the Senate, and the dominance of Quebec in federal policymaking has arguably been reduced. While fundamental aspects of the western critique remain unaddressed—a shift to a more open government through parliamentary reform, for example, has certainly not occurred—it is reasonable to presume that western dissatisfaction with the federal government has declined over time.

Survey data provide some empirical support for this assumption. The 2004, 2006, 2008,[9] and 2011 Canadian Election Study surveys all asked: "In general, does the federal government treat your province better, worse, or about the same as other provinces?"[10] When these data are used to track regional discontent over time, three conclusions are quickly apparent (see Figure 1.1). First, as expected, western discontent is generally declining: in all four western provinces, discontent as measured by this question fell by 20 percentage points or more from 2004 to 2011. The 2004 benchmark is an understandable high watermark in western discontent. In that election, which led to a Paul Martin Liberal minority government, western Canadians answering the survey question likely reflected not only upon the first six months of Paul Martin's leadership,

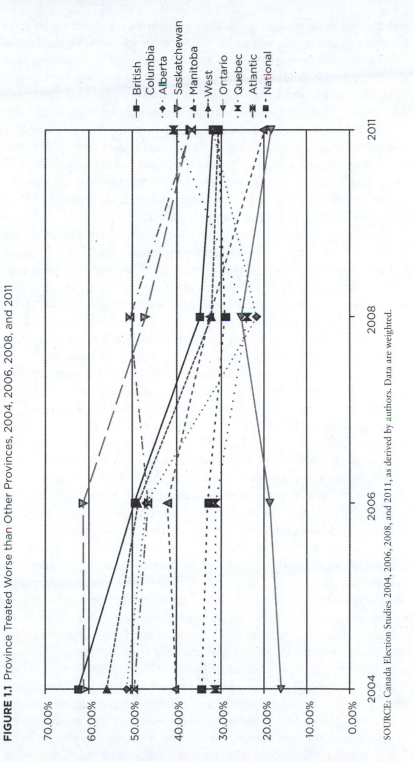

FIGURE 1.1 Province Treated Worse than Other Provinces, 2004, 2006, 2008, and 2011

SOURCE: Canada Election Studies 2004, 2006, 2008, and 2011, as derived by authors. Data are weighted.

but also on their perceptions of their province's treatment under Jean Chrétien's Liberal government between 1993 and 2003. Second, while Alberta has the reputation as the most discontented western province, this distinction in the survey data falls to Saskatchewan, followed closely by Alberta and British Columbia; Manitobans stand out as the least discontented. Third, unhappiness with the federal government is far from unique to the West. At the time of the 2011 CES, western Canadian discontent was very much in line with national feelings: just under one-third of all western Canadian respondents, and just under one-third of all respondents, felt that the federal government treated their province worse than other provinces. Indeed, regional discontent was *higher* in Atlantic Canada and Quebec than in the West.

This change in the temperature of western discontent should hardly come as a surprise given that the country's political leadership has shifted dramatically to the West, and the country's most Conservative electorate now enjoys a Conservative government. Electoral change also resulted in a dramatic increase in the proportion of western Canadian MPs who were part of governing caucus: over seven in ten western Canadian MPs in 2006, and over three in four in both 2008 and 2011 were on the government benches in the House of Commons. Thus, the election of the minority Conservative government in 2006 and the Conservative majority government in 2011 were highly significant events that signalled to the country, and to western Canadians, that the West was now in. As economist Mike Percy argues, "[i]t is very hard to be alienated when the prime minister is from Calgary and there are a number of very strong ministers from the West" (as quoted in Pitts 2011). Prime Minister Harper himself waded in on the night of his 2011 victory to say that the Conservative majority meant that "Western Canada can breathe a lot easier. . . . Some specific policies seemed to be almost targeted to do damage in Western Canada. It's a great thing those policies won't be coming to fruition" (Fekete 2011).

Another factor that *may* be contributing to declining western discontent is the region's changing demography, although here the empirical evidence is sparse. As Percy notes, "given the large interprovincial migration East to West, many Westerners are former Easterners. Alienation may still rear its head, but it is much less of a force" (as quoted in Pitts 2011). Rising immigration flows to western Canada may also have some influence, as Bilodeau, White, and Nevitte find that "[i]mmigrants from non-traditional source countries in Alberta and British Columbia supply significantly more favourable evaluations of the role played by the federal government than do Canadian-born respondents," although they go on to note what we consider to be an even more important point: "the fact that immigrants develop somewhat stronger federal loyalties than the Canadian-born population in their respective provinces does not imply that they are completely impervious to local dynamics. . . . In spite of the difference between immigrants and their corresponding Canadian-born provincial population, there is clear evidence of a strong reproduction of regional cleavages" (2010, 526, 533). Indeed, demographic growth in the West has always been fueled by in-migration from other parts of Canada and immigration from around the world, and neither has eroded regional discontent in the past.

While western discontent may be waning, regional conflict and discontent will never disappear in the very complex and heterogeneous Canadian federal state. As Percy suggests, regional discontent may be built into our national political economy:

> . . . because the structure of the Canadian economy is quite regionally specialized. If you look at the broad stereotypes, we have financial services in Toronto, manufacturing in the East, while it's resource-based in the West. And inevitably you have changes in terms of trade—the price of energy rises, for example—which create internal forces that cause real disparities in growth paths. That provokes responses in regions and the federal government is always stuck in the middle. Given the structure of the country, there will inevitably be regional tensions over the whole economic cycle. (As quoted in Pitts 2011)

At issue is not the eradication of regional discontent but rather its reduction to the point where the political system is not impaired. What, then, are the prospects for policy conflict in the new Conservative Canada, and in the inevitable post-Conservative Canada?

Starting first with the present Conservative government reality, and given both the Conservatives' political base in the West and the lessons of the NEP and the CF-18 decision, it seems reasonable to presume that the Harper majority government will take pains to avoid policies that are or appear to be unfair to western Canada. An example of this dexterity came with the October 2011 decision regarding National Defence shipbuilding contracts: shipyards in Halifax and Vancouver were awarded contracts of $25 billion and $8 billion, respectively, while the Quebec-based shipyard was not chosen. To avoid allegations of regional bias or unfairness, the decision was made through a non-political process; wrote the *Globe and Mail*'s Jane Taber, "Memories are still fresh, even though it happened back in the 1980s, of the repercussions that resulted from Brian Mulroney and his Progressive Conservative government awarding the CF-18 maintenance contract to Quebec instead of Winnipeg.

Stephen Harper's Tories don't need a repeat of that" (2011). (For a critical discussion about the independence of the delegated shipyard decision-making, see Howard [2011].) Thus, strong western representation within a Conservative majority government headed by a western Canadian prime minister can be expected to result in better protection of western Canadian economic interests, and either a non-partisan process (as was seen in the shipbuilding case) or due consideration of western Canada in the awarding of federal contracts.

At the same time, while western influence over government policymaking is certainly more pronounced than in the past, it still faces constraints. With 57 per cent of its caucus coming from outside the West, the Harper majority government will need to consider the political and policy interests of other regions, as any national government should, and the dynamics of cabinet-making in Canada virtually ensure greater regional balance in the cabinet than in the governing caucus. The Conservatives owe their majority status to Ontario as much as to western Canada. After the 2011 election, western Canada and Ontario had near-equal representation in the Conservative majority caucus, with 72 (43 per cent) and 73 (44 per cent) seats respectively. Conservatives from Atlantic Canada held 14 seats (9 per cent of the governing caucus), Quebec five seats (3 per cent) and the northern territories two (1 per cent). Given that the Ontario support may be seen as "softer" and more vulnerable in future elections, non-western Canadian interests should be expected to trump at times. Furthermore, while Prime Minister Harper is not reliant upon Quebec for his majority government—a profound change from majority governments of the past—both future electoral aspirations and longstanding national unity concerns necessitate due consideration of Quebec interests.

The challenge for the Harper government, then, is to balance its longstanding western Canadian support with its current Ontario support and the quest for future Quebec support—a challenging balance that has befuddled many previous federal governments. While majority governments of the past may have focused on balancing Ontario and Quebec interests, the new political landscape means that the federal majority government must now balance western Canadian, Ontario and Quebec interests. (How Atlantic and Northern interests will factor into this balance is uncertain.) The inclusion of western Canada in this "national balance" is an important development, but alone it does not mean that the West has a dominant role in the federation. While this is fair enough, it does mean that there remains the potential for a revival of western discontent even when the West enjoys strong representation in the federal government. (History here points to the heightened sense of western alienation during the second Mulroney government, as evidenced in the emergence and success of the Reform Party.)

The challenge of balancing regional interests across the country—of articulating an uncontested national interest—may well be matched by the challenge of balancing provincial interests and articulating a national interest within the West. For example, the federal government faces a formidable challenge in reconciling divergent Alberta and British Columbia perspectives on pipeline access to and tanker traffic along the west coast.

This brings us to our second question: will the contemporary decline in western discontent weather a future but inevitable change in the federal government? Given that federal policies so often provided the centrepiece of regional discontent, that dissatisfaction with Ottawa provided the regional glue for western Canada, it is important to consider what might happen if (or when) the composition of the federal government changes, when the federal government is again led by someone from outside the West. If the election of a Conservative government led by a western Canadian had such a dramatic impact on levels of regional discontent, what might be the impact of the next change in government? Will western Conservatives careen back to high levels of discontent, or will they be able to shrug off defeat, recognizing that you win some and lose some?[11] Governments will change—with Alberta being a possible exception!—and thus it is worth asking how dependent the West's new "attitude" is on being on the right side of the partisan fence. Will the region "slip back" into higher levels of regional discontent under a different government?

The answer, we suggest, depends on the rhetoric and actions of the government in question. It is possible to imagine a western Canadian future marked by a struggling resource-based economy, an outflow of population and diminished immigration, and an opposition party with charismatic leadership running against the West, appealing to voters elsewhere by arguing that the pendulum has swung too far to the West. Under such circumstances, or even under circumstances approaching this scenario, rising regional discontent would be inevitable. Admittedly, the political weight (number of seats in the House of Commons) and economic weight of the West are now so great that it is difficult to imagine how a national government could be formed without significant support from the western Canadian electorate. However, this is the case that used to be made about Quebec, that a national government without reasonable representation from Quebec would be both inconceivable and undesirable, and yet the Conservatives would have formed a majority government after the 2011 election without winning a single seat in Quebec. In recent years western Canadians have lived by the partisan sword, and the region is still not large enough to ensure that they will not die from it in future elections.

None of this is meant to be fear mongering for western Canadian readers. Rather it is simply to point out that things change, and the direction of change is unpredictable. If the West is now "in" only because of fortuitous partisan alignments and leadership, then we have to be careful about writing off the return of regional discontent in the future.

Conclusion: The West in Canada

In the introduction to this chapter we pointed to the powerful combination of economic conflict and fundamentally incompatible national visions. Now the first may be diminishing—it will never disappear completely—but the second is still very much in play. The economic conflict is about the place of the West within the federation, but the latter is more about the very nature of the national community.

It is easy to get the impression that western Canadians have faced unrelenting frustration and failure in their quest to reform the institutional status quo. Certainly the western vision has never had the national impact that the American western vision has had south of the border. In many ways, the western frontier in the United States came to define core American values, and the individuals who expressed those values on the screen—John Wayne, Gary Cooper, Ronald Reagan—became national heroes and symbols, central to American mythology and to how the United States is seen at home and abroad. There have been no counterparts from western Canada, although the CBC tries periodically to propel former Saskatchewan Premier Tommy Douglas into that role. Both inside and outside the United States, the American West *is America* in a way that the Canadian West *has never been Canada*.

After listening to western Canadian frustrations, foreign observers could be forgiven in reaching the conclusion that the last 50 years have been marked by constitutional initiatives designed to address Quebec's concerns, initiatives launched and stick-handled by federal prime ministers with a strong political base in Quebec. The West, such observers would conclude, has been ignored; western Canadians have been on the bench but not in the game. The reality, however, is much less bleak. In fact, we would argue that the West has had a major impact on Canadian political life. Supporting evidence for this argument can be found in the evolution of Canadian constitutional politics.

Since the late 1960s, Canadians have been engaged in a protracted constitutional debate, one that waxed and waned but never disappeared, and indeed may wax again with the resurgence of the Parti Québécois. Although the constitutional process has been largely if not entirely animated by the nationalist movement in Quebec, the constitutional changes that have emerged reflect a *western Canadian* constitutional vision. If anything, Quebecers have had much less success in the constitutional wars than have western Canadians. Consider, for example, the following:

- The decision in the 1970s to reject a bilingual/bicultural vision of Canada in favour of one that recognized bilingualism within a *multicultural* framework was very much an outcome driven by the West. Although biculturalism is fundamental to Canadian visions advanced from Quebec, it never captured the West's historical experience and its rejection as part of the national ethos was a clear "win" for the West.
- The 1982 Charter of Rights and Freedoms is, in many ways, only an elaboration and constitutional entrenchment of the 1960 Bill of Rights brought in by John Diefenbaker's Progressive Conservative government. Although an attachment to individual rights and equality is by no means unique to the West, it is deeply embedded in the region's pioneer past and contemporary political culture.
- The amending formulae in the 1982 *Constitution Act* embody the principle of provincial equality rather than any special or unique constitutional position for Quebec, whose veto power is no greater, and no less, than that of any other province. In this respect, the western Canadian provincial premiers, led by Alberta's Peter Lougheed, prevailed in a hugely important symbolic contest between provincial equality and special status for Quebec.
- The 1982 amending formulae did not provide a role for public consultation or consent; constitutional change was left in the trusted hands of governments. However, and at the insistence of the Reform Party, then a small opposition party, the approval or rejection of the 1992 Charlottetown Accord was put to a non-binding referendum and handily rejected. This precedent, although not constitutionally binding, may well be politically binding on any proposed major constitutional amendments to come. (Constitutional fine-tuning has been and remains possible without resort to referendum approval; an example here is the 1993 constitutional recognition of bilingualism in New Brunswick.)
- The notwithstanding clause in the *Constitution Act* was included at the insistence of Manitoba Premier Sterling Lyon.

- The *Constitution Act* provides additional recognition of and protection for the provincial ownership of natural resources, an issue that was central to the western Canadian premiers and of indifference to Quebec.
- The elaboration of Aboriginal rights in the *Constitution Act,* and in subsequent attempts at constitutional change, addressed an Aboriginal population that is largely resident in western Canada.
- The post-1982 constitutional debate at least opened the door for Senate reform, a goal strongly championed in the West and one that finds little but indifference and hostility in Quebec.

In summary, western Canadians made out like bandits in the extended constitutional process designed to address the place of Quebec in Canada. The new constitutional order, which we trace back to the Diefenbaker Bill of Rights, including his government's recognition of voting rights for registered Indians, seems to be stamped "Made in Western Canada."

Now, two formidable challenges remain. The primary reason we adopted a federal constitution in 1867 was to provide protection for the French Canadian (and Catholic) minority from the English Canadian (and Protestant) majority. In order to ensure that the national English majority could not be mobilized against the interests of the francophone minority, powers of particular importance to that minority, including education and civil rights, were assigned to provincial governments. Therefore the magic of federalism effectively transformed the francophone national minority in Canada into a majority within Quebec, where the conventions of majority rule posed no threat. Might, then, a redesigned federal system expand the western vision so that there is more space for Quebec? More specifically, could a more devolved federal state provide a workable bridge between Quebec and the West? Although western Canadians have not been strong advocates of greater devolution in the past, this may be an acceptable price to pay in order to create room for Quebec within a western Canadian constitutional vision. As matters now stand, that room does not exist, but in a free trade world, and with national governments focused more on economic management than social policy, it may well turn out that a federation tipped more toward provincial governments would fit the aspirations of both Quebec and the western provinces.

The second and quite likely more difficult challenge is to find a constitutional order, and a national vision, that more adequately includes Aboriginal peoples. To some extent this may come about through the courts, but this alone will not provide the foundation for a constructive partnership going forward. Although the issues here are national in character, not regional, the outcomes are of greater relevance for the West than for any other region. It is, therefore, a political conversation that calls out for western Canadian leadership.

Notes

1   A very different approach is taken by Friesen (1984).

2   The survey fieldwork for the Canadian Election Study was conducted by the Institute for Social Research (ISR) at York University. The principal co-investigators for the 2011 CES were Patrick Fournier, Fred Cutler, Stuart Soroka, and Dietlind Stolle. The Institute for Social Research, Elections Canada, and the Canadian Election Survey Teams are not responsible for the analyses and interpretations presented here.

3   The survey questions asked respondents "How do you feel about Canada?" (scale of 0 to 100), "Which do you prefer: a strong federal government, or more power to the provincial government?" and "Which government has the most impact on your life?"

4   Brian Mulroney's Progressive Conservatives won more seats in 1984, but a smaller proportion of the total seats in a larger House of Commons.

5   In the 1940s the Conservative Party changed its name to the Progressive Conservative Party in an effort to capture the progressive vote in western Canada, a strategy that bore little fruit until Diefenbaker came to lead the party.

6   In a related move, the Diefenbaker government also extended the federal franchise to Indians (to use the terminology of the times). Prior to 1960 only Indians who had enlisted in the Canadian forces, acquired a university degree or foresworn their Aboriginal status were allowed to vote in federal elections.

7   Respondents were asked to rate their feelings toward Quebec on a scale from zero "really dislike" to 100 "really like." Within western Canada, BC residents were the most positive about Quebec (mean = 68.2, similar to Ontario and Atlantic Canada), followed by Manitoba residents (63.5) while Alberta (56.6) and Saskatchewan (56.1) residents were notably less enthusiastic. Similarly, on the "do less" question, Manitoba (35.7 per cent "do less") and BC (35.0 per cent) residents hold less negative attitudes about Quebec than do Saskatchewan (44.4 per cent) and Alberta (48.1 per cent) residents.

8   The survey questions asked respondents "How do you feel about Quebec?" (scale of 0 to 100), "How much do you think should be done for Quebec?" and to state their level of agreement with the statement "We have gone too far in pushing bilingualism."

9   Data from the 2004 and the 2006 Canadian Election surveys were provided by the Institute for Social Research, York University. The surveys were funded by Elections Canada and the Social Sciences and Humanities Research Council of Canada (SSHRC), and were completed for the Canadian Election Survey Team of André Blais (Université de Montréal), Joanna Everitt (University of New Brunswick), Patrick Fournier (Université de Montréal), Elisabeth Gidengil (McGill University), and Neil Nevitte (University of Toronto). The fieldwork of the 2008 Canadian Election Surveys was conducted by the Institute for Social Research (ISR) at York University and the study was financed by Elections Canada. The principal co-investigators were Elisabeth Gidengil (McGill University), Joanna Everitt, (University of New Brunswick), Patrick Fournier (Université de Montréal), and Neil Nevitte (University of Toronto). Neither the Institute for Social Research, Elections Canada, nor the Canadian Election Survey Teams are responsible for the analyses and interpretations presented here.

10   The question, which goes directly to the issue of fairness, does have some limitations in assessing regional discontent; in particular, it asks about how the federal

government treats one's *province*, and not how the larger western, central, or Atlantic Canadian regions are treated. Further, it does not tap specific dimensions of regional discontent, such as the perception that one's province does not receive its fair share of federal revenue transfers. Nonetheless, the CES data have the advantage of allowing for comparisons between individual provinces (all provinces are treated as distinct in the CES surveys), and for tracking changes over time.

11 We are *not* suggesting that the Conservative government might go down to defeat due *only* to increased opposition from outside the West. It is possible that western Canadian voters may switch their support because of ideological opposition to the government of the day, changes in party leadership, dissatisfaction with the government's fiscal management, or strong opposition to particular policy choices relating to such things as environmental management or trade policy.

2. Demography and the Future of the West in Canada

IN FEBRUARY 2012, Canadian news outlets highlighted an important new demographic reality, as revealed by the release of data from the 2011 Canadian Census. The *Globe and Mail* reported that "Canada's West grows as the East stalls" (Mamak 2012), claiming that "Canada's future is in the West" (Friesen and Curry 2012). The *National Post* asserted that the Census data "reaffirm once again that the West no longer wants in—it is in" (Press 2012). The PostMedia newspapers, including the *Montreal Gazette* and the *Calgary Herald*, described Canada as "a country that remains firmly in the grip of a westward shift in population power—one that will see growing political and economic influence from Western Canada" (Boswell 2012). And perhaps most poetically, the *Vancouver Sun* suggested that the new Census numbers indicate that "[t]he sun is rising on the West" (2012).

Two facts in particular caught the attention of Canadians. The first "new reality" concerned population growth: the 2011 Census demonstrated that the pace of population growth is greater in three western provinces—British Columbia, Alberta, and Saskatchewan—than in other provinces, including Ontario. The second "new reality" concerned absolute population: the 2011 Census data revealed that the combined population of western Canada (30.7 per cent) is, for the first time, greater than the combined population of Quebec and the four Atlantic provinces (30.6 per cent) (see Figure 2.1). In the words of demographer Frank Trovato, this marked a "shift in the centre of gravity to the West" (as quoted in CBC 2012).

What do these new demographic realities mean for Canada? Demography is hugely important for understanding the nature of the

FIGURE 2.1 Population Share of Canada's Regions, 2011

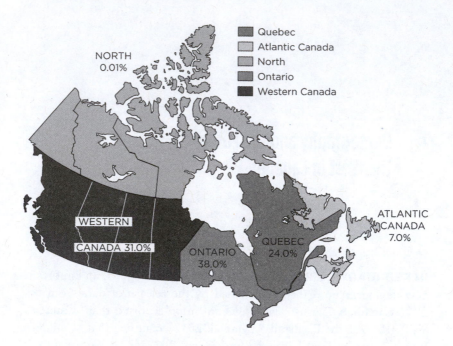

SOURCE: Statistics Canada (2012a, 10); image adapted by authors.

western Canadian political landscape, the place of the West in Canada, and interprovincial variations within the region. As Edmonston and Fong explain,

> The East-West relationships have a demographic aspect to them because population movements have changed the provincial distribution of the population over the past century. If everyone lived primarily in Ontario and Quebec, as was the case in the early 1900s, there would probably still be national concerns with the West, but they would not be a pressing national issue. Indeed, the settlement of the Prairies and the continued recent growth of Alberta and British Columbia—the result of both internal and international migration—have redefined the role of western Canada in the national political debate and the East-West relationship. (2011, 5)

This chapter will trace the changing demographic position of the West in Canada, and consider ways in which the western Canadian population is unique from and similar to the population in other parts of Canada. The chapter will then address the implications of western Canadian demographics for the country as a whole, arguing that both the population shift to western Canada and the policy responses to this demographic reality have important implications for all of Canada.

A Growing West in a Growing Canada[1]

The recent population shift is not the first time that western Canadian population growth has outpaced that of other regions; as Roach writes, "The region grew by a whopping 410% between 1901 and 1931 while the rest of Canada grew by a more modest 54%" (2010, 5). By 1931, almost 30 per cent of Canadians called western Canada home (see Figure 2.2). Western Canada's population share then fell during and after the Great Depression, and the West did not begin to significantly increase its share of the national population until the 1970s. Unlike the growth at the start of the twentieth century, however, western Canada's population growth since 1971 has been relatively gradual, but consistent—a fact that may account for the "surprise" some Canadians felt with the 2011 Census results.

Coverage of the 2011 Census data emphasized how western Canadian population growth was "outpacing" growth in other regions and provinces, particularly Canada's most populous province, Ontario. It is important to keep in mind, however, that while the latter's growth *rate* declined in the 2006–11 period, Ontario continues to grow; indeed, as the *Toronto Star* asserted, "While Ontario lagged the west in population growth in percentage terms, in real terms it grew by 691,539 people, easily outpacing all three western provinces. In fact, Ontario's growth

FIGURE 2.2 Regional Share of the National Population, 1901–2011

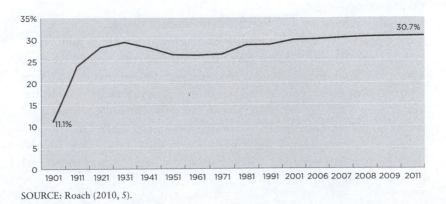

SOURCE: Roach (2010, 5).

alone almost equals the additional 706,701 people counted in Alberta (354,907); B.C. (286,570) and Saskatchewan (65,224)" (Campion-Smith 2012). Although this counting arguably undercounts the regional population—the reporter omitted Manitoba from his definition of the West, and with Manitoba's growth of 59,867 included, western Canada counted 766,568 additional people—the larger point that Ontario remains "central" (pun only somewhat intended) to the Canadian population is valid.

Current demographic projections suggest that western Canada will become home to an increasing proportion of Canadians in the decades ahead (see Ramlo, Berlin, and Baxter 2009; Statistics Canada 2010). As we will discuss later in this chapter, the increasing westward shift of Canada's population presents an interesting challenge to conventional conceptions of "Canada." Whereas in the past western visions of Canada lacked the demographic clout to transform the national debate, this is no longer the case. At the same time, Canadian history—and particularly western Canadian history—demonstrates that demographic fortunes can change unexpectedly, and here the West's relative drop during and after the Great Depression should serve as a cautionary tale for those who see current population growth as unrelenting.

Growing Faster through All Possible Means

What explains the rising population (in both proportionate and absolute terms) in western Canada? Populations change in three ways: natural change (natural increase, when births exceed deaths, and natural decrease, when deaths exceed births); internal migration (movement of citizens from one jurisdiction to another); and immigration (movement of non-citizens into the country). Western Canada's growth rate meets or exceeds those of other regions on all three measures.

Prairie Provinces and Quebec Lead "Natural" Population Change

Successful generational replacement in Canada would require a fertility rate of 2.1, with the fertility rate being the average number of children per woman. While none of the Canadian provinces have such a high fertility rate (Nunavut is the only jurisdiction that does), three western provinces come relatively close: Saskatchewan, Manitoba, and Alberta. Among the other provinces, only Quebec's fertility rate comes anywhere near that of the prairie provinces, while Ontario and British Columbia have Canada's lowest fertility rates. Overall, the three prairie provinces and Quebec stand out with respect to natural population growth.

BC, Alberta, and Saskatchewan Have Positive Net Internal Migration

Internal (or interprovincial) migration is a natural response to varying economic opportunities within a country. As Gauthier argues, internal migration can have national economic benefits:

> As long as different regions exhibit differences in employment rates and productivity and more people flow toward higher employment and higher productivity areas than in the opposite direction, these moves will generate net output gains at a pan-Canadian level. Voluntary internal migrations are therefore a "positive-sum game" that are desirable and will continue as long as sizeable regional economic disparities persist. (2011, 1)

Yet while the country as a whole may benefit, there are provincial "winners" and "losers" from internal migration: "For smaller provinces with low birth rates that struggle to attract sizeable shares of international immigration, interprovincial flows can mean the difference between economic renewal or stagnation" (Gauthier 2011, 1). Further, internal migrants tend to be younger, more highly educated and/or higher-income earners, and provinces that are net recipients of internal migration thus increase both the size of their skilled labour force and their prospects for natural increase (as younger residents are more likely to have children).

The current "winners" and "losers" from internal migration in Canada are clear. Over the past four decades, Quebec has had negative net migration, and Manitoba and the Atlantic provinces have experienced predominantly out-migration. Ontario, which had previously enjoyed in-migration, has seen negative or flat net migration for most of the 2000s. In contrast, British Columbia and Alberta have benefited from internal migration since 2003, and Saskatchewan has had positive net migration since 2007, all trends that are projected to continue in the short term.

The impact of internal migration on the western Canadian population cannot be overstated; while western Canada's immigration numbers have risen in recent decades, as will be discussed shortly, the development of the West is also very much a story about internal shifts in the Canadian-born population, as residents of central and Atlantic Canada have moved to the West. Further, internal migrants within the region are more likely to move to another western Canadian province (from Saskatchewan to Alberta, or from Manitoba to British Columbia, for example) than to a province outside the region. Thus the inevitable population churn within the national population works to increase the West's demographic clout.

Western Canada Attracts above Its Proportionate
Share of Immigrants

The primary destinations for immigrants to Canada are Ontario, British Columbia, and Quebec. However, in proportionate terms, the western Canadian provinces together attracted over 34 per cent of Canada's immigrants in 2008—above the region's share of the national population. This outcome can be attributed to the fact that two western Canadian provinces are "punching above their weight" in terms of immigrant attraction: British Columbia was the province of destination for 16.4 per cent of Canadian immigrants in 2008–2009, and Manitoba was the province of destination for 5.4 per cent. Indeed, Manitoba has been lauded for its immigration policies, which include partnerships with the Philippines, expansive settlement services, and an emphasis on immigrant retention strategies (Carter, Pandey, and Townsend 2010; CBC 2011; Kirby 2010; Prepost 2010). Further, it must be stressed that the data on the initial provincial destination of immigrants likely understate the importance of immigration to population growth in the West as immigrants tend to mirror the pattern of internal migration. A significant number of immigrants who land in other parts of Canada eventually head west.[2]

Western Canada's immigration gains have been Ontario's loss, as Ontario's share of immigration has declined by nearly 20 percentage points since 2001. These changes in immigrant location have consequences not only for provincial economies, but also for federal funding: "The shift hasn't gone unnoticed by the federal government. In 2012, Ottawa shifted its immigrant-settlement resources: Ontario services lost out, to the benefit of some of their Western counterparts" (Mehler Paperny 2011). Nevertheless, while Ontario's share of *recent* immigrants may be declining, the province remains home to the largest number and proportion of foreign-born Canadians.

There are two primary reasons why immigrants are increasingly electing to settle in western Canada. First, and as will be discussed more fully in chapter 3, Canada's economy and, as a consequence, job opportunities, have been shifting westward. Over the past decade, employment opportunities have been better in the West than elsewhere, and this has made the region a more attractive destination for immigrants. The second key factor is the provincial nominee programs, which are federal–provincial/territorial agreements that give provinces and territories a greater role in immigrant selection and recruitment. Provincial and territorial governments can use these agreements to help tailor immigration strategies to meet specific labour market needs. Analysts

FIGURE 2.3 Foreign-Born (Immigrant) Population by Province, 2011

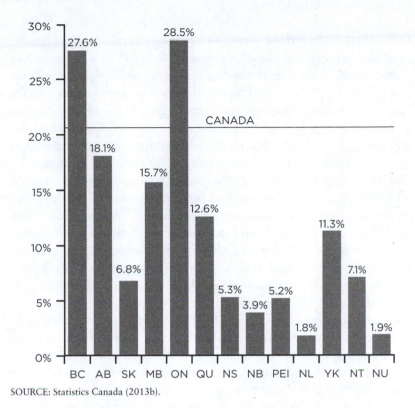

SOURCE: Statistics Canada (2013b).

point to the provincial nominee programs in particular when discussing Ontario's declining immigration numbers. Ontario was slow to take advantage of new program opportunities in the 2000s; as the *Globe and Mail* reports, "While provinces such as Manitoba, British Columbia and Alberta jumped at the newly created provincial nominee program early in the decade, Ontario did little. . . . The other provinces used the nominee program to gobble up applications, such as tradespeople, who don't fare well in the points system for skilled worker applications. As the skilled-worker stream declined, so did Ontario" (Friesen 2012).

These immigration patterns represent an important historical shift: while western Canada was the primary destination for immigrants before the Great Depression, for much of the mid-twentieth century immigrants generally ignored the region. This re-emergence of the West as a destination for immigrants—either those who first settle in the West, or those who initially settle in another region and then move west—has implications for all regions of Canada.

Population Shifts within Western Canada

While we have thus far considered western Canada's population in contrast to other regions, it is also important to consider the population distribution *within* western Canada. In the early twentieth century, the regional population was relatively evenly distributed among the four western provinces and, in 1931, Saskatchewan—yes, Saskatchewan!—was the regional leader, with a population approaching one million. Indeed, Saskatchewan was Canada's third most populous province, after Ontario and Quebec. At that time, British Columbia had the smallest population in western Canada, and was only the sixth largest province in Canada. Over time, Saskatchewan and British Columbia have effectively swapped positions, both in terms of regional and national population weight; as of 2011, British Columbia was Canada's third largest and western Canada's largest province, while Saskatchewan was Canada's sixth largest and western Canada's smallest province. Further, the former relatively balanced distribution of population within western Canada has given way to a region that heavily tilts westward. While British Columbia and Alberta enjoyed continuous population growth between 1971 and 2011, Saskatchewan and Manitoba alternated between periods of growth and decline, and the once-dominant Saskatchewan in particular struggled with reversing provincial out-migration. It is only since 2007 that all four western provinces have enjoyed steady population growth. The growth rate in Saskatchewan and Manitoba in recent years is of note; Saskatchewan enjoyed Canada's third highest growth rate (after Alberta and British Columbia), and Manitoba's growth rate doubled from the previous intercensal period. These shifts in growth rates represent considerable change: as Statistics Canada writes, "The increased [national population] share of the Western provinces since 2006 is essentially due to the population growth of the Prairie provinces, whereas, in the past, it was mostly attributable to the growth of British Columbia" (2012a, 10).

Although Saskatchewan and Manitoba are now growing in absolute terms, their demographic weight within western Canada remains light compared to that of Alberta and British Columbia; as of 2011, 42.8 per cent of the region's population lives in British Columbia and 35.4 per cent in Alberta, with only 10 per cent of the regional population residing in Saskatchewan and 11.7 per cent in Manitoba. This has important implications for the West as a political community, as the interests of Alberta and British Columbia within the region loom larger and larger.

Looking beyond Growth: Population Characteristics[3]

While western Canada's population growth is notable in and of itself, it is also important to recognize that the western Canadian population differs from the national population in some key ways. These differences, which are in some cases modest and in other cases quite striking, will have relevance for public policy, politics, and perhaps even the evolution of the Canadian national identity.

Western Canada's Population: More Urbanized than the Postcards Suggest

There is little doubt that Canada is an urban nation. In 2011, almost 7 in 10 Canadians lived in one of the nation's 33 Census Metropolitan Areas (CMAs), each of which has a population of at least 100,000, and another 13 per cent lived in one of Canada's 114 Census Agglomerations (CAs), which have populations of at least 10,000. Of the remaining population, almost 5 per cent lived in a rural area close to a CMA or CA (e.g., in the outskirts of an urban area), with only 14 per cent of the Canadian population living in "rural" areas remote from a CMA or CA, and less than 1 per cent (0.2 per cent) living in the territories.

Perhaps due to its agricultural past and vast lands, western Canada continues to invoke visions of rural landscapes and vast open areas. However, these associations run contrary to demographic realities, for it is Atlantic Canada that stands out as having the largest rural population: 44.7 per cent of Atlantic Canadians live in rural areas, compared to 19.4 per cent of Quebecers, 14.1 per cent of Ontarians, and 18.5 per cent of western Canadians. Western Canada's (perhaps unexpectedly) small rural population reflects urbanization rates in British Columbia and Alberta; as the Urban Futures Institute observes,

> while British Columbia is commonly portrayed as a rural province, and Ontario as an urban one, in fact, a (marginally) greater percentage of BC's population lives in urban areas than in Ontario. . . . In a similar vein, while the common image of Alberta is of farms and ranches dotted with oil wells, [Alberta is] Canada's third most urban province behind BC and Ontario. (2008, 1)[4]

Saskatchewan (33.2 per cent) and Manitoba (27.6 per cent) continue to have considerably higher rural populations than do British Columbia (13.8 per cent) and Alberta (16.9 per cent), highlighting important demographic differences within the region itself.

Given the stronger population growth in western Canada overall, it is not surprising to learn that western Canadian CMAs had particularly strong growth rates between 2006 and 2011, with all western Canadian CMAs except Winnipeg and Victoria exceeding the national average. If Canada's future is, as many commentators suggest, an urban future, this is no more apparent than in the West.

Western Canada's Population: Not Just Faster Growing, but Also Younger

As is the case in most industrialized countries, Canada's national population is aging. Over time, fertility rates have decreased; mothers are having children later in life, thus slowing generational replacement; and Canadians are living longer. The result is that both the age of the average Canadian and the proportion of seniors (aged 65 and older) in the population are rising over time, while the proportion of children (0–14) and working-age (15–64) Canadians is declining. This does not mean that the number of children and working-age Canadians is declining in absolute terms, but rather that the growth rates of these cohorts (0.5 per cent and 5.7 per cent, respectively between 2006 and 2011) does not come near to matching the growth rate of seniors (14.1 per cent). Indeed, Statistics Canada's "medium growth scenario" projects that by 2016, for the first time in Canada's history, the number of seniors in Canada will be greater than the number of children.

Although population aging is a fact for all provinces and regions, the pace of population aging is considerably faster in Quebec and Atlantic Canada than in Ontario, western Canada and the territories. This is true not only because of the higher fertility rates in western Canada, but also because of interprovincial migration as young people are more likely to move than are mid-career and older people. Immigration patterns make an additional contribution as "the age profile of the immigrant population is markedly younger than the resident population" (Ramlo, Berlin, and Baxter 2009, 10). Together, the three demographic growth trends (fertility, internal migration, and immigration) have resulted in different age profiles for provinces across Canada. Between 2006 and 2011, the proportion of children declined in Atlantic Canada, Ontario, British Columbia, and the NWT, rising only in the three prairie provinces and (marginally) in Quebec; the proportion of "working-age" people declined in Atlantic Canada, Quebec, and (marginally) the Yukon while rising in Ontario, western Canada, the NWT, and Nunavut; and the proportion of seniors increased in all provinces and territories except Saskatchewan. As a result of these differing trends, median ages across Canada vary considerably, with the median age of residents in the territories and the prairie provinces being considerably lower than the average age of residents in Atlantic Canada.[5] Assuming that patterns of immigration and internal migration remain constant, and given that younger populations are (or will become) the parents of Canada's next generation, these regional age disparities are likely to sharpen in the years to come.

Western Canada's Population: Ethnically and Culturally Diverse, but Dissimilar to Central and Atlantic Canada

For the past four decades, if not longer, Canadians have celebrated the multicultural nature of their society. As discussed in chapter 1, multiculturalism initially reflected the frontier reality of western Canada when early settlement upset the existing Canadian demographic applecart as immigrants poured in from Scandinavia, Russia, the Ukraine, Poland, and other Eastern European countries. Canada became multicultural through the settlement of the West where Canada's original bicultural blueprint was overlaid by a new immigrant population; Canadian diversity would never be the same. Later, Canadian policy and, ultimately, national identity became multicultural when western Canadians led (successfully) the resistance in the early 1970s to Canada being officially described as a bilingual and bicultural society.

While Canada's multicultural roots were laid and nurtured in the West, western Canada does not necessarily have a reputation for cultural diversity. For many, "western Canadian" brings to mind images of (white, male) cowboys, farmers, and loggers—and perhaps, for some, of Aboriginal peoples. Toronto, with its strong representation of a wide range of cultural backgrounds, is broadly seen as the home of Canadian ethnic and cultural diversity. Yet, as the following discussion will demonstrate, western Canada is also home to considerable diversity, although this diversity differs in important ways from the diversity found in Ontario, Quebec, and Atlantic Canada.

Aboriginal Peoples Are an Important and Growing Segment of the Western Canadian Population

The importance of Aboriginal peoples to the western Canadian population, and the importance of western Canada to Canada's Aboriginal peoples, must not be overlooked. Aboriginal peoples are a key—and growing—component of the regional population. Further, Aboriginal peoples—including First Nations, Métis, and Inuit peoples—are constitutionally recognized and have both unique rights and unique social challenges.

FIGURE 2.4 Distribution of Canada's Aboriginal Population, 2011

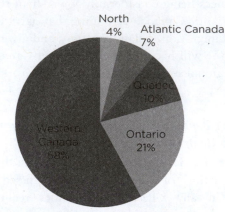

SOURCE: Statistics Canada (2013a), as calculated by authors.

Nearly 6 in 10 Aboriginal people in Canada live in the West (see Figure 2.4). The region's Aboriginal population is spread relatively evenly across the four western provinces, and British Columbia and Alberta are home to greater numbers of Aboriginal peoples than are Saskatchewan and Manitoba in absolute terms. However, due to the fact that Saskatchewan and Manitoba are smaller provinces, Aboriginal peoples constitute a much higher proportion of the Saskatchewan (15.6 per cent) and Manitoba (16.7 per cent) populations than the Alberta (6.2 per cent) and BC (5.4 per cent) populations.

Western Canada Has Fewer Refugees and More Asia–Pacific Immigrants than Other Regions

Canada has three main immigrant categories: economic immigrants, family class immigrants, and refugees. Individuals who have the "ability to become economically established in Canada" may apply as economic immigrants, those with a familial relationship to a Canadian citizen or permanent resident may apply as a family class immigrant, and individuals who are among "the displaced and the persecuted" may apply as refugees (Justice Canada 2001, c. 27, 12[1–3]). The distribution of immigrants from these categories varies across Canada. In 2010, only 5.5 per cent of western Canada's permanent residents were refugees—a figure considerably lower than the national average—and both western Canada and Atlantic Canada had a proportion of economic immigrants that was considerably higher than the national average. Ontario, in contrast, had a higher proportion of family class immigrants and refugees among its permanent residents (Citizenship and Immigration Canada

TABLE 2.1 Immigrants to Canada in 2010 by Source Area

2010	AFRICA/ MIDDLE EAST		ASIA/PACIFIC		SOUTH/ CENTRAL AMERICA		UNITED STATES		EUROPE/UK	
	#	%	#	%	#	%	#	%	#	%
Canada	66,693	23.8	135,005	48.1	28,354	10.1	9,243	3.3	41,319	14.7
Western Canada	14,175	14.1	63,490	63.3	5,637	5.6	3,179	3.2	13,756	13.7
ON	28,836	24.4	58,852	49.8	12,032	10.2	4,715	4.0	13,633	11.5
QU	22,020	40.8	8,070	14.9	10,393	19.3	1,002	1.9	12,492	23.1
Atlantic Canada	1,627	20.8	4,228	54.0	279	3.6	318	4.1	1374	17.6
Northern Canada	35	6.9	365	72.1	13	2.6	29	5.7	64	12.6

SOURCE: Citizenship and Immigration Canada (2010).

2010). Regions also differ in the source categories for immigrants. In 2010, 6 in 10 immigrants to western Canada were from Asia-Pacific countries, with other provinces receiving more immigrants from Africa, the Middle East, South America, and Central America (see Table 2.1).

Four Out of Canada's Five Most Diverse Cities Are in Western Canada

Population diversity is most evident in large cities, with 96 per cent of Canada's visible minority population living in CMAs in 2011. (The official definition of "visible minority" in Canada is set out in the *Employment Equity Act*: "persons, other than Aboriginal peoples, who are non-Caucasian in race or non-white in colour.") While Toronto has the largest visible minority population in relative terms (47.0 per cent of Toronto residents are visible minorities), Vancouver (45.2 per cent) is almost equally as diverse. In Montreal, a city often celebrated for its multiculturalism, 20.3 per cent of residents are visible minorities, below Calgary (28.1 per cent) and Edmonton (22.4 per cent) and just above Winnipeg (19.7 per cent).

Western Canadian Populations Are among the Most Diverse in Canada

Overall, when one considers population diversity as encompassing both visible minority and Aboriginal populations, the western Canadian provinces are clearly among the most diverse in Canada (see Figure 2.5).

FIGURE 2.5 Population Diversity by Province, 2011

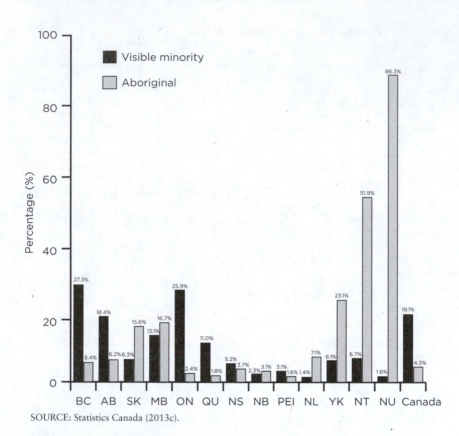

SOURCE: Statistics Canada (2013c).

Ethnic and cultural diversity is considerably lower in Quebec and Atlantic Canada.

Western Canadian Linguistic Diversity Is Not Reflective of Official Bilingualism

While Canada is both officially and in the aggregate bilingual, with a mixture of English and French, western Canada is not. As the West was settled, the linguistic make-up of Confederation-era Canada was not replicated in western Canada: migrants from Quebec went to the New England states rather than to the West, and the West emerged as a very different linguistic region than Canada as a whole. Although official bilingualism, introduced in 1969 by the *Official Languages Act,* facilitated increased bilingual education and bilingual product labelling across Canada, it in no way altered the linguistic realities of western

Canadian demographics. As of 2011, very few western Canadians identified French as their mother tongue (1.5 per cent for British Columbia, 2.1 per cent for Alberta, 1.7 per cent for Saskatchewan, 3.8 per cent for Manitoba)—considerably below the rates of Quebec residents reporting English as their mother tongue (8.3 per cent). (In Ontario, 4.1 per cent report French as their mother tongue, compared to 32.0 per cent for New Brunswick, 3.6 per cent for Nova Scotia, 3.9 per cent for PEI, and 0.5 per cent for Newfoundland and Labrador.) This is not to say that English is the exclusive mother tongue in western Canada; indeed, many western Canadians report primary languages other than English. However, the other primary languages reported are not French: 27.3 per cent of BC, 20.1 per cent of Alberta, 13.2 per cent of Saskatchewan, and 22.4 per cent of Manitoba residents report a non-official language as their mother tongue—rates that not only reflect the cultural diversity of western Canada, but also (with the exception of Saskatchewan) approach or (in the case of British Columbia) exceed the rate of non-official primary languages in Ontario (26.6 per cent).

Summary

Western Canadian population growth is relevant to the future of Canada not just because of the locational shift in the national population, but also because there has been a shift in the composition of that population. Simply put, the western Canadian population does not replicate the central Canadian template. The age profile is somewhat different. Ethnic and cultural diversity has a different face in the West. And linguistic diversity in western Canada in no way reflects Canada's official English-French bilingual status. These differences, we argue, have consequences for public policy, for politics, and for our ever-changing understanding of what it means to be "Canadian."

Implications: Demography, Politics, and Public Policy

In their popular book, *Boom, Bust and Echo*, David Foot and Daniel Stoffman assert,

> Demographics explain about two-thirds of everything. . . .
> If more of our decision-makers understood demographics,
> Canada would be a better place to live because it would run
> more smoothly and efficiently. . . . It is simply not possible to do
> any competent planning without a knowledge of demographics.
> (Foot and Stoffman 1998, 8, 9)

Strong words, but we shall try to heed their warning. What do demographics—and, more particularly, the varying demographics between western Canada and the rest of Canada, and within western Canada—mean
for Canadian politics and public policy? It is our contention that they have
significant implications across the country.

Political Implications of Western Canadian Demography

One might think that western Canada's population growth would result
in growing political weight in federal politics. However, this growth has
been slow to translate into increased representation in the House of
Commons where the redistribution of seats is legislatively set to occur
only once every decade, after the decennial census. Further, for a number of reasons (see Sancton 2010; Mendelsohn and Choudhry 2011),
provincial seat allocations within the House of Commons deviate from
the principle of representation by population. By 2011, Ontario suffered
the greatest under-representation, and British Columbia and Alberta
were also underrepresented relative to their populations (Mendelsohn
and Choudhry 2011).

After the 2011 election, the federal government introduced and
passed the *Fair Representation Act* that established a new seat allocation formula for the House of Commons. By the time of the 2015 federal
election (assuming electoral redistribution timelines are met), the House
will increase in size to 338 seats, with 15 new seats for Ontario, 6 new
seats for each of British Columbia and Alberta, and 3 new seats for
Quebec. The new seats mean that BC's weight within the House will
increase from 11.8 per cent to 12.5 per cent of the total seats while
Alberta will maintain its current level of representation (10.1 per cent of
House seats) (DeSouza 2011).

What does this change mean for western Canada? The proportionate weight of "the West" within the House of Commons will be largely
unchanged: prior to the *Fair Representation Act* the West had 29.9 per
cent of the total House seats, and moving forward the West will have
30.8 per cent of the seats. That said, the symbolic importance of this
change should not be understated. As discussed in chapter 1, a long-
standing narrative of political under-representation has informed western regional grievances over the decades, and this grievance has now
been addressed. Further, while the seat changes will have a relatively
minor impact on the composition of the House of Commons, they do
underscore the broader perception that political weight in Canada is
shifting west. We will return to consider the political implications of this
change in chapter 6.

Population change may also alter the ongoing Senate reform debate.
As noted in chapter 1, western Canadians (and particularly Albertans)

have long supported Senate reform, and in particular the proposal for a Triple E Senate in which the reformed Senate would be "equal, elected, and effective." In June 2011, the *Senate Reform Act* proposed guidelines for voluntary provincial Senate elections and nine-year term limits for new senators. Interestingly, western Canadian critiques of the Senate reforms promoted by Stephen Harper's Conservative government focus on the Act's failure to address the disjuncture between the regional distribution of Senate seats (which reflects population patterns at the time of Confederation and the subsequent addition of provinces) and the current distribution of the population, suggesting a move away from provincial equality as a guiding principle. Future discussions of Senate reform, to the extent that they occur, will likely place greater attention on the distribution of seats. In light of population shifts to the west, and west within the West, the logic of an "equal" Senate may well be losing its appeal, particularly in British Columbia and Alberta, and arguments for Senate abolition, rather than reform, may be gaining momentum.

The varying demographic conditions of provinces and their interplay with provincial and regional economies also have potential implications for regionalism in Canada. Regionalism refers to "a set of attitudes and feelings: an identification with an area; a sense of a certain distinctiveness from other areas; an attachment to a territory, its people, and institutions" (Breton 1981, 58–59). While regionalism can be politically benign, it can also energize and shape the political system if residents of some regions feel politically disadvantaged relative to other regions, a theme that we discussed more fully in chapter 1. It is not difficult to imagine a wide range of issues—including climate change, employment insurance reform, equalization, immigration, resource development and market access, trade negotiations, and temporary foreign workers— that are or could prove to be regionally divisive. Here Beaujot and Kerr write, "The economic 'core' of Canada, especially Toronto and Montreal but more broadly the Windsor-Quebec corridor, has established itself as the centre of Canada, providing both a source of unity in its large population and of disunity owing to resentment from outlying parts of the country" (2004, 133). It is our contention that the growing demographic and economic weight of the West presents a rival "centre" that, should it be sustained, will transform our discussions about national unity and disunity.

Public Policy Implications of Western Canadian Demography

Somewhat paradoxically, the strengths of western Canada's demography mean that some of the most challenging national public policy questions of the next decade will emerge with greatest force in the West. Urbanization is one example. Growing cities enjoy greater opportunities for urban renewal and change, but at the same time rapid population growth in many western Canadian cities presents a policy challenge with respect to the need for infrastructure and the management of urban sprawl. Like cities across Canada, cities in the West face challenges of infrastructure development, maintenance, and renewal, and these challenges become more urgent in the face of rapid growth. In Edmonton, "[y]oung families flock to the city's multiplying subdivisions, leaving officials scrambling to deliver schools, emergency services and transit. Suburban schools are filled beyond capacity as soon as they open, while inner-city schools are threatened with closing due to low enrolment" (Friesen and Wingrove 2012). Although the management of urbanization is unquestionably a policy issue for all provinces, it will play out with greatest effect in western Canada.

Population aging is another issue that affects all provinces, but with some regional variations of note. While population aging might be seen as the positive result of health care advancements and societal prosperity, there are broad concerns about its implications for labour supply; simply put, at some point in the not-too-distant future, the number of individuals entering the workforce will be insufficient to replace the number of individuals retiring. A shrinking labour force has implications in turn for the economy and for federal, provincial, and territorial tax bases. There are also concerns about health care and other social services: the growing population of seniors is anticipated to increase health care costs, and governments may be hard-pressed to maintain current levels of health care services and other social supports. As Banerjee and Robson summarize, "Canadians increasingly worry that demographic change threatens their future living standards. This concern is well placed" (2009, 1).

Part of the Canadian dilemma, and an important complication when considering a national policy response to an aging population, is that the policy challenges of population aging do not play out evenly across Canada. In the short term, population age profiles present western Canada with some advantages, while the declining growth of the child and working-age populations and the increasing growth of the seniors population in Atlantic Canada suggest significant long-term challenges. In the words of the *Globe and Mail*'s David Campbell, "this demographic tsunami is hitting Atlantic Canada first and this region has far less capacity to address it than the rest of Canada" (2011). At the federal level, the government will need to balance regionally different needs with regard to pension and employment training policies, among other issues. At the provincial level, governments will differ with respect to fiscal capacity, education policy, and health care demands.

These provincial variations are brought into focus by the concept of dependency ratios. A province's dependency ratio refers to the ratio of the combined youth population (0 to 19 years) and senior population (65 or older) to the working age population (20 to 64 years). It is expressed as the number of "dependents" for every 100 "workers." In a rough way, dependency ratios relate to the sustainability of public programs as they capture the balance between taxpayers and those who tend to draw most heavily on many social programs, particularly the young and old; in this way, lower dependency ratios present provinces with some advantages. In 2011, British Columbia and Alberta, along with Newfoundland and Labrador, enjoyed the lowest dependency ratios among Canadian provinces; dependency ratios were also relatively low in the Yukon and Northwest Territories. At the same time, western Canada has the country's highest provincial dependency ratios in Saskatchewan and Manitoba, so clearly the West's advantage on this issue is specific to British Columbia and Alberta (Statistics Canada 2012g).

We have argued that western Canada is an ethnically and culturally diverse region, albeit in ways somewhat different from the rest of Canada. What are the policy implications for the region? Looking first at the Aboriginal population, it is well-documented that Aboriginal Canadians participate less in electoral politics and the wage economy and have considerably poorer socio-economic outcomes than non-Aboriginal Canadians. The concentration of Aboriginal peoples in the West means that the future of Canada's Aboriginal population will play out, in large part, in western Canada. Of course, other provinces share western Canada's interests in assisting and empowering Aboriginal peoples—indeed, more Aboriginal people live in Ontario than in any single western Canadian province, and the challenges facing Aboriginal peoples should be and are a concern for all Canadians. At the same time, western Canadians have a particularly strong interest in creating a positive future for Aboriginal peoples. As western Canada is home to a large and growing Aboriginal population, addressing the disparities between Aboriginal and non-Aboriginal Canadians is a critical policy challenge. The western Canadian provincial governments are well aware of the importance of this issue; examples of policy efforts on this front include Manitoba's "Closing the Gap" initiative and the importance of Aboriginal peoples to labour-market strategies in the western provinces. Greater success in addressing the needs and interests of Aboriginal peoples is essential for the sustainability of a resource-based economy that is thoroughly entangled with Aboriginal land and land claims.

What are the policy implications of the rising diversity in western Canada through immigration? Although a number of countries have experienced social cohesion challenges in the face of increased immigration and diversity, this has not been the case in Canada: "immigrants to Canada come from such a wide range of source countries, and they also have such widely varying cultural and religious backgrounds, that accommodation of the differences becomes the norm" (Picot 2011, 29). Indeed, research finds that "[t]he longer new immigrants are in Canada, the more their sense of pride and, to a lesser extent, of belonging comes to equal or exceed that of the largest ethnic group. Thus, the integrative power of Canadian life for newcomers is impressive" (Soroka, Johnston, and Banting 2007, 23). Overall, then, while western Canada might be expected to experience policy challenges with respect to immigrant settlement and foreign credentials recognition, it should also be anticipated that growing diversity due to immigration will help define the region in positive terms, as rich social diversity has done for Toronto and Montreal.

Western Canada's immigrant profile is distinct from other regions, with the western provinces having proportionately fewer refugees and more economic class immigrants. Given the differing needs and training levels of individuals in different immigrant categories, these regional differences are not without policy consequence: Ontario and, to a lesser extent, Quebec, may be facing some of the greatest challenges associated with immigration, while other regions enjoy more of the benefits. Further, research suggests that immigrant class has relevance: economic immigrants tend to earn more (Abbott and Beach 2011, 2) and have higher self-reported health status (Zhao, Xue, and Gilkinson 2010, 19), and the Canadian general public is more supportive of economic immigrants than family class immigrants and refugees (Citizenship and Immigration Canada 2012, 6). For these reasons, immigration policy debates may have different emphases in western Canada than in other regions.

Does the fact that western Canadian immigrants tend to come from different source countries matter? Arguably, yes: the robust Asia-Pacific population in western Canada may well present the region with an economic advantage in the years ahead. As will be discussed further in chapter 5, the global economy is increasingly shifting toward Asia, and Canadian governments are striving to increase trade with the Asia-Pacific countries. The West's Asia-Pacific immigrants could be a very important bridge in the future as Canada's economy, and the global economy, centre more and more on Asia.

A final important demographic difference between western Canada and other regions (particularly central Canada) is the fact that French is an uncommon mother tongue in the West; linguistic diversity in the region does not reflect the national policy of official bilingualism. In light of this linguistic reality, it is perhaps no surprise that official bilingualism lacks broad popular support in western Canada. Official bilingualism attempted—and continues to attempt—to impose a linguistic template for Canada that is not reflective of western Canada's past or current demographic realities, and in the years ahead there may be regional differences in support for the continuation of official bilingualism and/or for maintaining current levels of French services offered at the provincial level, should such issues become part of active policy debate.

Many of these demographic differences, and policy responses to them, have potential implications for the evolution of national identity, which has been at least in part, if not primarily, a product of deliberate public policies (Bashevkin 1991; Brodie 2003; Béland and Lecours 2008). In the past Canada's national identity was largely forged by efforts to accommodate the bilingual and bicultural realities that Quebec represented, and thus the resulting identity was more "central Canadian" than "western Canadian." Increasingly, however, the centrality of Quebec to Canada's national identity, and economy, is eroding, and Ontario's dominance in defining "English Canada" has been weakened. This raises the possibility that western Canadian visions of Canada, as discussed in chapter 1, may gain greater traction in the years ahead.

Conclusion

The social, political, and policy relevance of demography is unmistakable. The growing western Canadian population and the changing composition of that population are important not only for the future of western Canada, but also for the future of Canada as a whole. How Canadians come to grips with demographic change and its implications is no small matter, and it will help to determine our country's future. Some suggest that demographic change will result in long-lasting political transformation; for example, the *Globe and Mail*'s John Ibbitson (2012) argues that demographic shifts, combined with economic change, have altered Canadian politics in a fundamental way:

> There are now too many people and there is too much money in the West for it to be ignored. Just as no party could once have expected to form a majority government without sufficient

support in Quebec, today a majority government depends on
support west of Lake of the Woods. The values and priorities of
the West are now national priorities. This is permanent.

Yet, at the same time, it is important to recognize that this is not the first
time Canada's population has shifted westward, and Canadian demographic history demonstrates that growth patterns can certainly change.
The West's current share of the national population is approximately
the same as it was in 1931, and it is entirely possible that, just as in the
1940s and 1950s, the West's share of the population may drop in the
face of economic change. The importance of the economy to the West's
demographic future cannot be overstated, and it is to that topic that we
now turn.

Notes

1 The data presented in this section are drawn from Statistics Canada (2009, 2012a,
   2012d, 2013b); Roach (2010); Gauthier (2011); Milan (2011a, 2011b); Beaujot
   and Kerr (2004); Basavarajappa and Ram (2012).
2 Statistics Canada's 2011 National Household Survey finds that 35.6 per cent of
   "newcomers" (those who immigrated to Canada between 2006 and 2011) resided
   in western Canada: 15.9 per cent in British Columbia, 12.4 per cent in Alberta, 2.3
   per cent in Saskatchewan, and 5.0 per cent in Manitoba.
3 The data presented in this section are drawn from Statistics Canada (2012a, 2012c,
   2013a, 2013b, 2013c, 2013d) and Roach (2010).
4 While the Urban Futures Institute reported 2006 data, the same pattern is observed
   with the 2011 data.
5 The median age in the prairie provinces ranges from 36.5 years (Alberta) to 38.4
   years (Manitoba), while the median age in Atlantic Canada ranges from 42.8 years
   (PEI) to 44.0 years (Newfoundland and Labrador). The national median age is
   40.6 years (Statistics Canada 2012d).

3. The West and Canada's Shifting Economic Centre of Gravity

IN MAY 2012, comments by Thomas Mulcair, Quebec MP and leader of the Official Opposition, provoked spirited debate about western Canada's contribution to the national economy. Mulcair argued that natural resource industries were driving up the value of the Canadian dollar, and that Canada's manufacturing sector was suffering as a consequence of the high loonie. In his words, "The Canadian dollar's being held artificially high, which is fine if you're going to Walt Disney World, [but] not so good if you want to sell your manufactured product because the American clients, most of the time, can no longer afford to buy it" (as quoted in Abma 2012). The West, far from being the "engine of the Canadian economy," was being portrayed as sand in its gears.

Not surprisingly, Mulcair's comments drew quick fire. Some (particularly economists) challenged Mulcair's belief that Canada was suffering from "Dutch disease," a situation in which strong resource markets and high costs within the resource sector drive up the value of the exchange rate to the point where it hurts international export markets for the manufacturing sector, as happened, albeit briefly, in the Netherlands in the 1970s. Others focused on the regional nature of his argument. The natural resource industries that he accused of driving up the Canadian dollar are heavily concentrated in western Canada, while the manufacturing industries that he argued are being hurt, such as the automotive sector, are heavily concentrated in central Canada. Mulcair, critics charged, was playing the classic Canadian political game of pitting one province or region against another.

Mulcair was not the first to advance the "Dutch disease" argument; Ontario then-premier Dalton McGuinty beat him to it, making (and then very quickly retracting) the argument a good two months prior. However, given that Mulcair was the leader of the Official Opposition, and therefore a national figure aspiring to be prime minister, his comments sparked the most vigorous response. More fundamentally, and critical to the analysis to follow, Mulcair hit upon *the* central question in any discussion of the West's position within the national economy: should Canadians embrace resource extraction as our niche within a highly competitive global economy, or should we—and particularly western Canadians—be moving away from resource extraction, and perhaps toward the economic model represented in the recent past by Ontario? How Canadians react to the changing economic circumstances in western Canada, and to Mulcair's Dutch disease thesis, depends very much on whether resource extraction is seen as Canada's past or future.

Where one stands on this question will be determined in part by where one sits within the national economy. In a country as vast as Canada, strong regional differences in industrial structure and economic interests are inevitable. Indeed, Canada's national economy often seems little more than a loosely integrated set of quite divergent and sometimes competing provincial economies, knit together by a common currency and geographic proximity. Some provinces, such as Ontario and Quebec, enjoy geographic advantages in terms of easy access to key American markets, just as British Columbia may in terms of proximity to Asia. Other provinces, such as Alberta, Saskatchewan, and Newfoundland and Labrador, enjoy natural resource advantages in terms of oil and natural gas, while still others, such as British Columbia, Manitoba, and Quebec, enjoy natural resource advantages with respect to the ability to generate hydroelectric power. The importance of these various advantages will change over time and with a variety of factors, many of which are beyond Canada's control. But given the differing economic bases of Canada's provinces, it is of little surprise that provinces and regions vary considerably in their economic interests, and that the articulation of these interests inevitably becomes political fodder.

This chapter traces the changing economic position of the West in Canada, and considers ways in which the western Canadian provincial economies are different from the provincial economies found in other parts of the country. In so doing, we demonstrate that Canada's economic fortunes are increasingly dependent on the success of the western Canadian provincial economies and argue, therefore, that western Canadian economic interests are—or should be—of interest to all Canadians. We also argue that the volatility of the West's natural resource economies in the face of international pricing, fluid national policies, and growing public concern (both local and global) about environmental impact, mean that provincial and federal governments alike need to carefully address specific western Canadian economic policy issues.

Western Canada's Growing Economic Weight in Canada[1]

In March 2012, *The Economist* argued that, just as Europe faced the spectre of a "two-speed Europe," Canada was developing into a "two-speed north":

> Ontario is Canada's hobbled manufacturing heartland, which has suffered not just from relative economic stagnation but also from a rising currency. CIBC World Markets, an investment bank, projects its GDP will increase by just 1.7% this year. In contrast, the bank forecasts Alberta and Saskatchewan, two western provinces enjoying energy booms, to grow by 3.3% and 3.1%.

The magazine went on to note that "[m]any of the benefits of that [western] expansion accrue to the federal government" (*The Economist* 2012).

The Economist (and CIBC, upon whose economic forecasts it relied) is not alone in singling out western Canadian provinces. In 2011, 2012, and 2013, the Conference Board of Canada predicted that western Canadian cities would lead urban economic growth in Canada, with Saskatoon heading the pack (Abma 2011; Conference Board of Canada 2012; Lu 2013). In May 2012, BMO Economics reported that "[w]hile the Canadian economy continues to grow at a moderate pace, there is a widening gap between commodity-rich Western provinces and the manufacturing-heavy provinces in Central and Atlantic Canada" (2012a). In March 2013, RBC Economics' provincial economic forecasts highlighted the "natural resource–intensive provinces" of Newfoundland and Labrador, Alberta, Saskatchewan, and Manitoba (Ferley, Hogue, and Cooper 2013). The emerging consensus is that the western Canadian provinces are an increasingly important part of the national economic picture; indeed, some go so far as to argue that they are *the* most important part.

The relative strength of the component provincial economies in the West (economic data are seldom aggregated for the region as a whole) is seen across a number of measures. Chief among these is gross domestic product (GDP). In nominal terms, western Canada's GDP has grown in both absolute and proportionate terms over the past decades. As of 2011, the West accounted for 36.5 per cent of national GDP—considerably above its population weighting, and above its 31 per cent contribution to national GDP in 1999.[2] Further, a number of organizations predict that western Canadian GDP growth will outpace that of other regions in the near future. BMO Economics summarized the national situation thusly: "The resource sector continues to fuel growth in Western Canada. . . . Central Canada continues to be bogged down by an array of challenges, including fiscal restraint, an above-parity loonie and sluggish U.S. demand . . . [and] the strong loonie and a period of subdued public-sector capital spending have depressed growth in Atlantic Canada" (2012b, 1).

Other measures also point to regional economic strength. Western Canada accounts for a considerably higher proportion of Canadian total international exports than its population would suggest. The unemployment rate in all four western provinces is below the national average, and the labour market participation rate for the three prairie provinces exceeds the national average. Western Canada has emerged as a leader in private and public sector capital investment: in 1991, 32 per cent of Canadian capital investment was made in western Canada, whereas by 2012 this had grown to over 45 per cent.

The proportion of corporate head offices located in the region further demonstrates the growing economic importance of the western provinces. Toronto, of course, remains home to the greatest number of corporate headquarters: in 2009, 265 of Canada's 800 largest corporations had their head offices in Canada's largest city. At the same time, the major western cities together were the site of 284 of Canada's largest corporate head offices, with the lion's share—114—being located in Calgary. While Toronto's importance as Canada's corporate home is by no means threatened, the growing number of western-based corporate head offices speaks to the region's increased economic contribution to Canada, and to the belief within the corporate sector that this contribution will continue to increase. Indeed, the book cover description for Gordon Pitt's *Stampede! The Rise of the West and Canada's New Power Elite* (2008) reads: "Above all, *Stampede!* is about business leadership and how it is changing right across the country. It zeroes in on the corporate leaders in Alberta who will set the business and social agenda in Canada for decades to come. For Canadians outside Alberta, this is an introduction to their new bosses." Clearly, in the eyes of some Canadians, the West will play a growing role in Canada's corporate future.

Overall, the economic data converge to illustrate at the very least a gradual, incremental westward shift in the country's economic centre of gravity, not a stampede but a steady drift now decades old. At the same time, it must be recognized that there is considerable risk in using current snapshots of measures such as GDP and employment rates to make future projections. Predicting long-term economic trends is particularly precarious in the case of western Canada where the relative strength of the regional economy depends very much upon volatile international commodity prices. The markets for coal, gas, lumber, oil, potash, and wheat can shift quickly and dramatically, as provincial finance ministers know so well. This reality raises an important question: is the West's current economic growth sustainable? In other words, is the West's relative strength within the national economy a short-term blip or does it reflect structural changes likely to endure? To answer this question we must turn first to a somewhat more detailed discussion of the region's economic underpinnings.

Understanding Western Canadian Economic Interests

Western Canada is endowed with a resource base that is the envy of most nations. There are substantial high-grade deposits of minerals including copper, gold, lead, molybdenum, silver, uranium, and zinc, along with some of the world's largest potash deposits. The region is not only Canada's primary source of oil, natural gas, and coal, but it also has huge hydroelectric capacity in British Columbia and Manitoba. The rich prairie soil is the nation's major producer of grains—wheat, barley, oats—as well as producing forage and pulse crops, oil seeds, potatoes, and sugar beets. The more arid parts support substantial herds of cattle and feedlot operations for both cattle and hogs. The northern temperate rainforests of coastal British Columbia, together with the inland boreal forests stretching across the top of the region, provide the bulk of Canada's production of softwood lumber and pulp and paper. Given this resource base, it is not surprising that western Canada has a predominantly export-driven natural resources economy; while this is particularly apparent in Alberta and Saskatchewan, natural resources are also very important to British Columbia and Manitoba. Further, the service and manufacturing sectors in the four provinces are highly integrated with the natural resources sector, building around the core of resource extraction.

Although the regional economy is far from homogeneous, either across or within individual provinces, the four western provinces have shared economic interests that to a significant degree are unique to the region. For perhaps obvious reasons, transportation capacity is of particular concern to western industries and businesses; market access is essential, and most markets are distant. (As we will discuss shortly, market access challenges increasingly reach well beyond infrastructure.) The centrality of resource-based industries to the provincial economies also means that international trade issues are highly relevant to the region, and that international market fluctuations can have significant impact on the economic fortunes of individuals, firms, and provincial treasuries. Analogous factors for the central Canadian economy would include the St. Lawrence Seaway and the greatly improved access it provided to European markets, and the 1965 Auto Pact that secured or at the very least protected Canadian access to the American automotive industry.

The Importance of Transportation Systems

Western Canada is a vast area. With 2.9 million square kilometres of space, the four provinces together are "almost large enough to hold 7 Californias or 12 United Kingdoms" (Roach 2010, 54). Moreover, much of the area is sparsely populated. While it is true that Canada as a whole has a low population density, with the large majority of the population living in urban centres relatively close to the American border, western Canada's population density (3.6 persons per square kilometre in 2009) is considerably lower than that of Atlantic Canada (4.3 persons per square kilometre), Quebec (5.1), and Ontario (12.1). The combination of a relatively sparse and small population—the total population of the four western provinces is roughly equivalent to that of metropolitan Chicago—and plentiful natural resources means that the regional economy is by necessity an export-driven economy. The domestic market is simply too small to absorb the West's resource production, a fact that holds true today for oil, timber, and uranium just as it held true in the past for furs and wheat. In the wake of this basic reality come a number of challenges.

While the relatively empty areas are filled with natural resources, profiting from these resources requires access to often distant markets. Cattle, grains, hogs, lumber, natural gas, oil, potash, sulphur, uranium, and other resources must be moved by train, truck, pipeline, airplane, and/or ship for processing and sale. For much of Canada's history and continuing to this day, the United States has been a key market for Canadian goods. And while Ontario, Quebec and, to a lesser extent, the Atlantic provinces enjoy relatively close proximity to American population and economic centres, the western provinces abut less densely populated states that are also producing many of the same commodities that western producers are trying to sell—there is a limited Montana market for Canadian grain, or North Dakota market for Canadian oil. In short, western Canadian products must travel greater distances to reach their markets—even American markets.

Western Canada's transportation infrastructure—its airports, highways, pipelines, ports, and railways—provides the foundation for the regional economy, the essential linkages to distant markets. As a sparsely populated, extremely large land mass located at the geographic margins of the national and continental economies, western Canada is highly dependent on its transportation network. If the region's goods do not move efficiently, it adds costs to producers, costs that if ultimately passed on to consumers would make the West's goods less competitive. Even e-commerce and service industries are dependent on transportation to move their goods—or, at the very least, to supply the computers upon which their commerce is based.

Given this reality, western Canadian governments and producers have had (and continue to have) a keen interest in national and provincial transportation policies. Yet while efficient transportation systems—both north-south and east-west trade corridors—would appear to be essential strategic investments for the region, this is a policy area where the West has been a relatively poor performer, and where federal-provincial policy coordination has been weak. The provincial transportation systems are not well integrated, and public funding (federal and provincial alike) for infrastructure has been inconsistent and episodic. Infrastructure development is very expensive in the region: in addition to the sheer distances to be covered there is the complicating matter of weather. In the prairie provinces and BC's interior and northern areas, extreme temperature fluctuations (temperatures below -30°C in the winter and above +30°C in the summer) place strains on transportation infrastructure. The overall point to stress is that the transportation costs for western Canadian producers and governments are considerable, and the political fact is that, when push comes to shove, it is easier to cut funding for transportation infrastructure than it is to cut spending in other areas such as health care and education. Infrastructure spending, it seems, can always be put off until next year, or the next. The West is not unique in facing this political reality, but it is a challenge nonetheless.

Here it is also worth noting that important parts of the infrastructure puzzle lie in private hands, and are therefore more difficult targets for public investment. Railroads, pipelines, and airports, for example, are private rather than public utilities, and although they are certainly influenced by the regulatory hands of government, they are very different in character than the highway system. Electrical power in British Columbia, Saskatchewan, and Manitoba is delivered almost exclusively through Crown corporations. To make a complex situation even more complex, many of the critical infrastructure challenges are found within large urban centres, thus bringing municipal governments and local interests into play. (Here capacity and access challenges for the Port of Vancouver provide striking examples.) Although the importance of infrastructure to the regional economy is readily admitted, effective policy responses can be elusive.

The Joys and Frustrations of Resource-Based Economies

Natural resource industries are heavily dependent upon trade; producers export their products to other, typically international, markets. Given this emphasis on export trade rather than on inter-provincial trade, on export markets rather than domestic markets, it is not surprising that western Canadians were (and remain) among the chief proponents for liberalized international and internal trade (Berdahl 2013). An export-based economy, unlike a manufacturing economy servicing domestic markets, cannot be protected by tariffs and non-tariff barriers to trade.

In addition to generating a keen interest in trade policy, dependency on international trade has another implication for the western provinces. The international prices received for natural resource products can fluctuate greatly. Such fluctuations are perhaps most visible with respect to oil prices where unavoidable international fluctuations can be exacerbated by bottlenecks and price differentials within the continental economy. For example, in 2013 the Alberta government's budgetary forecasts had to be dramatically revised due to falling prices for bitumen despite relatively robust international prices for oil, a phenomenon described by Premier Redford as the "bitumen bubble." This volatility is also present for other resource prices as well, including copper, natural gas, uranium, potash, and lumber. As price "takers" rather than price "setters" in the global economy, the western provinces can go through dramatic periods of "boom" and "bust" due to shifts in international demand and prices, and unlike OPEC they cannot fix the price of exported commodities by adjusting supply. This boom-bust cycle has important implications for provincial budgets as revenues from natural resources are inherently less stable and predictable than are government revenues from income and consumption taxes. Furthermore, highly publicized "world prices" for commodities such as oil can give an exaggerated picture of regional wealth, for dependency on a single American market can mean that the price producers receive is markedly lower than the world price. In recent years, for example, the price for Western Canada Select, the regional benchmark for low quality, viscous heavy oil, has often fallen to less than 50 per cent of the world benchmark, a distinction that is not always picked up by external commentators on the western Canadian economy.

The emphasis on resource development also means that western Canada's provincial economies are unavoidably entangled with Aboriginal land and communities. Resource developments, and the roads, rail lines, and pipelines that move resources to international markets, inevitably and appropriately bring Aboriginal interests into play. Accommodating those interests in a way that meets constitutional requirements for consultation, is congruent with Aboriginal rights and values, and provides tangible economic benefits for Aboriginal peoples is an ongoing challenge that, to date, has been met to only a modest extent. Creating the frameworks for full and enduring partnerships has been very difficult.

A final and increasingly important challenge for resource-based economies is balancing resource extraction with environmental stewardship. Finding this balance and ensuring that the quest for prosperity today does not damage the environmental legacy for future generations are particularly difficult issues for western Canada. This balance was brought into focus in 2002 by acrimonious debates about the implementation of the Kyoto Accord and, more recently, by national and international controversies surrounding the Alberta oil sands. In the years to come, the environmental agenda will only expand: climate change, water and air quality, water supply in the face of drought and urban growth on the prairies, sustainable forestry, and endangered species are just some of the issues that will require both public policy solutions and astute political management. Crosscutting all these specific and difficult environmental challenges is the over-arching question of governance: who should determine the appropriate balance between environmental protection and resource extraction? What are the appropriate roles for the provincial and federal governments, and for Aboriginal governments? What happens if governments differ with respect to where that balance should be struck?

In summary, an ongoing reliance on natural resources gives a distinctive cast to western Canada's provincial economies. However, it is also important not to exaggerate this regional distinctiveness. Although the resource sector looms large in western Canada, it is far from absent in other regions. Consider, for example, the northern Territories, Newfoundland and Labrador, the mineral riches of northern Ontario, and the potential for shale gas and oil in the St. Lawrence Valley. Aboriginal communities are thoroughly entangled with resource developments in western Canada, where the great majority of the Aboriginal population lives, but they are also major players in resource developments in Ontario's "ring of fire" and in developments, including hydroelectric power, in northern Quebec and Labrador. And even though the western Canadian provincial economies, and for that matter the national economy, are heavily dependent on exports, across all regions, including the West, more Canadians by far are employed in the service sector than in any other sector; most Canadians work in retail trade, education, health care, and financial services.

The specific economic differences between the West and other regions, therefore, are largely ones of degree rather than kind. However, when they are all taken together, a unique regional economy, a true difference in kind, can be seen. And, we would argue, albeit with somewhat less certainty, the differences *among* the four western provinces are less than the differences between the West and the rest.

Public Policy and Western Canadian Economic Interests

In January 2012, Saskatchewan Premier Brad Wall argued that the structure of the federal Employment Insurance (EI) program hurts Saskatchewan. According to Premier Wall, EI is a program that "discourages Canadians from moving here. In some regions, a person can work just over 10 weeks and receive almost a year's worth of EI benefits. A worker in Regina will work roughly twice as long for significantly less. Yet, employees and employers pay identical premiums into this $22-billion a year program" (Taber 2012). Wall also argued that the federal equalization program, one resting on constitutionally entrenched principles if not details,[3] creates disincentives for labour mobility in Canada. Wall called on the federal government to rethink federal policies so to better deal with labour shortages in some provinces and regions.

Premier Wall's comments illustrate a central theme in our analysis: while there has been increased market liberalization in some areas in recent decades, the capacity of western Canada to adjust to and thrive within the current and future economic environment will still be determined in part, and perhaps in large part, by public policies, both provincial and federal. In this section, we outline policy implications for the western Canadian provincial economies. Given the reciprocal relationship between regional and national prosperity, we argue that both provincial governments in the West and the federal government are key actors in addressing the region's economic challenges. Without specific attention to the region's economic needs, ongoing problems will be left to fester, thus imperiling the prospects for regional *and national* prosperity within an increasingly competitive global environment.

We consider three specific policy areas: trade, labour market development, and economic growth and diversification.[4] In doing so, we place considerable emphasis on the role of the provincial governments who hold many important economic policy "levers." As Hale writes, "The legal and political structures of federalism have contributed to the regional differentiation of Canada's economy by giving provincial governments control over economic development policies and transportation systems within their provinces, the ownership of national resources, and the political incentive to use those powers to promote the economic well-being of people and businesses within their territory" (2006, 224). The importance of provincial policy to provincial economies has arguably increased over time: although any impetus toward greater decentralization of the Canadian federal system has historically been tempered by the federal spending power,[5] cuts to transfer payments in the 1990s meant that provincial governments assumed even greater responsibilities for their residents' economic well-being. Given these realities, it is important to consider what steps the western provincial governments can take to advance and protect their economic futures.

Although federal policy remains relevant, as Premier Wall's arguments about EI and equalization suggest, the dynamics of globalization predict that national governments will become less relevant to citizens over time as much of their existing policy capacity will be lost to (or embedded within) international agreements such as NAFTA and those issued by the World Trade Organization (WTO), to markets, or to more localized political authorities. The expectation in this line of thinking is that powers presently in the hands of national governments will shift up to international agreements, down to provincial governments, or out to markets, leaving "hollowed out" national governments at the sidelines of major public policy debates. To some degree this trend can be observed in Canada, and more specifically in the economic relationship between the federal government and the West. While federal policy had considerable influence over the western economy in the past (as discussed in chapter 1), circumstances are considerably different in the twenty-first century. In a more free trade environment, and particularly within the context of NAFTA, western Canadian producers have direct access to American and global markets that is increasingly unmediated by the federal government. (The critical role of the federal government in negotiating such free trade agreements will be discussed in chapter 5.) While rail, air, road, and sea linkages between the West and global markets remain critically important, federal programs have less and less to do with such linkages—federal spending on transportation infrastructure is modest (although the various gateway and US border infrastructure initiatives should not be overlooked), airports have been privatized, and federal regulatory frameworks have largely given way to market competition. Whether this is a desirable state of affairs is an important question in its own right, but there is little doubt that for better or for worse, a well-established trend points to a diminished federal role.

As a consequence of these changes, actions or inactions by the federal government have less capacity to assist or harm a regional economy characterized more and more by strong north-south and global ties, and comparatively weaker east-west ties. Yet to say that Ottawa counts for less is *not* to say that it counts for naught, and therefore an important question remains: are the residual national programs of net benefit to western Canada as the region adjusts to new economic realities? As Ottawa wrestles with Canada's changing position within the North American and global economies, it may pursue policies on issues such as supply management, airline competition, and climate change that will adversely affect regional interests. Admittedly, the federal government in the future will be more constrained in its capacity to influence the western Canadian provincial economies for good or for ill. At the same time, when we look more specifically at the conditions for economic prosperity in western Canada, it is clear that the policies and programs of the Government of Canada still have considerable bite. The federal government's domestic policies may be of less importance than in decades past, but its international policies are becoming more important over time.

Policies to Foster and Expand Trade

As a producer of natural resources, western Canada has always been a trading region, be that trade international or internal. We will discuss international trade at length in chapter 5, and here shall limit our discussion to internal trade.

While internal trade has not grown at nearly the same rate as international trade, the fact remains that internal markets are still important to western Canada. Indeed, the "western provinces exported $117.2 billion worth of goods and services within Canada in 2008, which is equivalent to 19.4% of the region's GDP" (Roach 2010, 114). Almost 50 per cent of the western Canada's interprovincial trade is internal to the region itself, a reality that points to an extensive intra-regional economy and speaks to the need for reduced internal trade barriers and an efficient regional transportation system. The western provinces—or at least three of the four western provinces—have made some progress in addressing internal trade barriers within the region. As will be discussed further in chapter 4, in 2006 British Columbia and Alberta signed the Trade, Investment and Labour Mobility Agreement (TILMA), an agreement designed to reduce interprovincial trade barriers. In 2010, Saskatchewan was added to the agreement, which was renamed the New West Partnership Trade Agreement (NWPTA). These are important steps to strengthen the internal regional economy, even though to date they fail to include Manitoba. NWPTA goes considerably further in reducing internal trade barriers than does the pan-Canadian Agreement on Internal Trade (AIT), and demonstrates the West's capacity for national policy leadership. Moreover, the AIT includes exceptions that allow for continued internal trade barriers (see Berdahl 2013). Moving forward, the western provinces may wish to advance the continued liberalization of internal trade, although here we must note that some internal barriers may by necessity be removed as a condition of international agreements (Berdahl 2013).

Is there room to significantly expand internal trade in Canada? Economists estimate that the costs of internal trade barriers are low, and therefore the reduction in trade barriers over time is unlikely to have a large impact on internal trade flows. However, an exception that has been raised in recent years is the potential for greater internal trade in oil. Historically, western Canadian oil flowed into Canadian markets west of the Ottawa River, and into the United States. Quebec and Atlantic markets were supplied primarily from offshore sources including the North Sea, Venezuela, and the Middle East. As a consequence, Canada has been a major oil exporter *and* importer. Now, as American markets for Canadian oil weaken in the face of growing American supply and falling American consumption, and as Asian market access remains difficult, there is increased interest among some western Canadian producers in enhancing the country's east-west pipeline capacity in order to replace imported oil in eastern Canada with the western Canadian product, thus keeping upgrading and its associated employment within Canada. The Irving oil refinery in New Brunswick, which is Canada's largest, could serve Canadian, American, and offshore markets. If regulatory approval and provincial government support can be secured, it would be a rare example of internal trade displacing a significant piece of international trade.

Many of the initiatives to strengthen the internal market reflect the assumption that a significant *regional* economy exists, that it makes sense to think of western Canada as an economic region characterized by a fair measure of interdependence. Nonetheless, it would be a mistake to overstate public or political buy-in to regional models. In an interview with the *Globe and Mail* during the 2013 BC election campaign, Premier Christy Clark acknowledged the national importance of the western Canadian economy, arguing that "they [Central Canada] need us now more than they ever have . . . because we [as a country] are not in a period of economic expansion and they cannot do it without us." However, Clark went on to address the Northern Gateway and Kinder Morgan pipeline proposals in decidedly non-regional terms: "The pipelines that are of most interest to British Columbians are liquefied natural gas. That's something we can do and we don't need the federal government and we don't need Alberta. We can do this ourselves and make this contribution to our country and our province without their help" (Hunter 2013). Clark's eye was fixed resolutely on the creation of an LNG industry in her province, one whose feedstock would be found in British Columbia and whose markets would be found in Asia.

Policies to Address Labour Market Needs

Due to both labour market demand and population aging, the West along with the rest of the country faces a serious challenge in the years ahead in terms of labour supply and tax base. Public policy has a role to play with respect to increasing the number of immigrants coming to and remaining in western Canada, increasing Aboriginal engagement in the regional economy, and attracting and retaining the young skilled workers who are so integral to the increasingly knowledge-based economy. Public policy also has a role in ensuring that western Canada's post-secondary system—including universities, colleges, trade institutions, and apprenticeship programs—meets the future training needs of the region. Taken together, these facts speak to the need for a strategic approach to the development of human capital, one that mobilizes the resources of both the federal and provincial governments.

Challenges relating to labour supply and the development of human capital take us to core provincial responsibilities for education, health care, and social services. Provincial governments play a key role in training the future workforce, retaining the working age population (and particularly skilled labour), and attracting workers from other provinces and internationally. In some cases—training workers, recognizing credentials from other jurisdictions, providing immigrant support services—the policy implications are quite clear. In other areas, and particularly the attraction and retention of workers, the role of provincial policy is both broader and less clearly defined, encompassing such factors as quality of life, tax rates, and employment opportunities.

Although the federal government plays a less comprehensive role, it can also influence in a number of ways the growth of the labour market and the strength of human capital. One key labour market policy area in which both the federal and provincial governments play a role is immigration, an area of concurrent federal–provincial jurisdiction.

The federal government determines the total number of immigrants coming into the country, the mix of immigrant classes, the criteria for immigration, the size and conditions of the temporary foreign workers program, and the ceiling for the number of immigrants allowed to each province under the provincial nominee programs. The federal government is also heavily involved in settlement support and language training (delivered through provincial and private institutions). Where provincial governments have the capacity to excel is in immigrant retention—for example, keeping immigrants to Saskatchewan in Saskatchewan—and the attraction of immigrants from other provinces (e.g., attracting immigrants initially settling in Ontario to move to and settle in Manitoba). The role of effective immigrant settlement services and strategies is demonstrated by Manitoba's considerable success in this regard, as noted in chapter 2; the province's pioneering work in establishing provincial nominee programs has carried through with Manitoba's disproportionate engagement. Moving forward, the western provincial governments may work to enhance their immigrant settlement programs, and to encourage the federal government to re-examine its allocation of immigrant funding. Here we point specifically to Quebec's entitlement to 25 per cent of new immigrants (a target never met) and 25 per cent of federal funding (a target that is met), a policy that fails to meet any standard of common sense when viewed from a national economic perspective.

Training is another area for policy consideration. Provincial post-secondary institutions speak to labour market capacity; while not all jobs require post-secondary education, many do, and the need for post-secondary training—be it a university degree or a technical or trade certificate—will only grow in the years ahead as Canada and other countries move toward a more knowledge-based economy. Provinces with a higher proportion of educated individuals in their workforce may enjoy economic advantages with respect to the size of the skilled labour force and potential tax base, given that employment rates increase with educational levels and higher education attainments are often (albeit not perfectly) related to higher income levels.

A 2012 Statistics Canada report shows that western Canada does not enjoy any particular advantage with respect to educational levels; that advantage lies with Ontario. Indeed, Saskatchewan faces a considerable challenge on this front (Statistics Canada 2012e). The lower than average rates of higher education in Saskatchewan may reflect both the relatively high proportion of Aboriginal residents (Aboriginal Canadians are less likely than non-Aboriginal Canadians to complete post-secondary education) and the province's long and only recently reversed history of population out-migration. Since the Great Depression in the 1930s, tens of thousands of provincial residents, particularly young people, have left the province after the completion of their post-secondary training, leading some pundits to argue that "people" were among Saskatchewan's greatest exports.

Governments can take a number of steps to support and grow a skilled labour force. The first—and most obvious—step is to support the provision of post-secondary education and training, including training in skilled trades. Although the federal role here is constitutionally subordinate to that of provincial governments, federal agencies—primarily the "Tri-Councils" of the Natural Sciences and Engineering Research Council of Canada (NSERC), the Social Sciences and Humanities Research Council of Canada (SSHRC), and the Canadian Institutes for Health Research (CIHR), as well as the Canada Foundation for Innovation (CFI)—are the major funders of research in post-secondary institutions, and the funding decisions they make and the themes they choose to pursue in large part determine the national and global competitiveness of these institutions.

A second and perhaps less obvious step that governments can take is to ensure that prospective students—primarily but not exclusively young people—have the capacity to succeed in post-secondary education and training. Of particular concern here are high school dropout rates, especially among young males and Aboriginal peoples, and the need to ensure that Aboriginal students have the social supports, educational backgrounds and life skills necessary for post-secondary success. One critical area for federal engagement is addressing both the social and educational disparities experienced by on-reserve First Nation populations.

A third consideration for labour market strategies, and one that receives considerably less attention than others, is examining how federal and provincial policies structure the incentives (and disincentives) for retirement. In the face of labour shortages, it may be necessary to rethink retirement incentives, considering instead how policy can create incentives for older western Canadians to stay engaged, even on a part-time basis, in the work force. This is a dramatic shift from public policy thinking of the past. Canada's labour system is based on the assumption of oversupply of labour. While this assumption may have been appropriate in the past, it could not be more inappropriate for current and future realities. The federal government's decision in 2012 to move the onset of Old Age Security support from age 65 to age 67 is an example of policy adaptations, or in this case program adaptations to a changing demography and labour market.

These first three points—investments in education, addressing the needs of Aboriginal peoples, and creating incentives for delayed retirement—apply across Canada, are not unique to the West (although Aboriginal initiatives apply with greater force in the West), and are unlikely to engender much in the way of regional or interprovincial conflict. However, a fourth and final suggestion to address labour market needs in western Canada is bound to be more contentious, and that is taking policy steps to enhance internal migration. As noted in chapter 2, internal mobility is a fact of life in Canada, and a prerequisite for an adaptive economy. But, while the net effect nationally is argued to be positive, there are inevitably "winners" and "losers" at the provincial level; unlike immigration, internal migration is a zero-sum demographic game. The challenge for the federal government is to encourage greater labour mobility, with its positive impact on the national economy, while remaining neutral in the inter-regional competition for human capital, which is difficult given that the impact of federal programs is seldom uniform across the country. National policies in the past, including EI eligibility criteria, have been designed to countervail market forces encouraging mobility; that is what regional economic development programs are all about. Although it is unlikely in the near future that Canadians and their governments will abandon a tradition of trying to move jobs to people rather than encouraging people to follow employment opportunities across provincial lines, this dedication is not conducive to regional and national prosperity.

Provincial policies are also important in creating incentives or disincentives for internal mobility. In the past, Canada faced problems with trade credential recognition across provinces; despite the stated goals of the Agreement on Internal Trade, interprovincial barriers in skills transferability were a national problem and embarrassment. The provincial and territorial governments have addressed this to a certain degree with the new AIT labour mobility chapter, introduced in 2009 (Berdahl 2013). Thus, the key steps that western Canadian provincial governments can take to promote internal migration centre on quality of work and quality of life factors—as well as favourable tax environments—the very same steps needed to retain existing skilled labour in the provinces.

Policies to Support Economic Growth and Diversification

Since the introduction of the National Policy in 1879 (see chapter 1), public policy has been designed to ensure that Canadians would be more than "hewers of wood and drawers of water," and by and large Canada was successful in building a modern industrial economy. Success, however, was less evident in western Canada, and particularly in Alberta,

Saskatchewan, and British Columbia, which remained relatively dependent on resource extraction and agriculture, and as a result they were afflicted with booms and busts brought on by highly variable global markets. (Manitoba, with its more diversified economy, has experienced less dramatic effects from resource price volatility.) Governments responded in turn with largely unsuccessful diversification strategies. Today, however, Canada's manufacturing heartland is increasingly under threat by the same global competition that is driving up demand for western Canadian resources. Suddenly the hewers and drawers are doing very well, but concerns remain about the need for and mechanics of economic diversification.

Despite years of pursuing the holy grail of economic diversification, the western provinces remain heavily dependent on the export of price-volatile resources and agricultural commodities.[6] This dependency comes with a significant downside, as Western Economic Diversification explains:

> Dependence on natural resources makes Western Canada vulnerable to risks such as volatility in the commodity markets, disruptions from trade disputes and disasters, and environmental issues. Whereas the rest of Canada generates a greater proportion of GDP from the manufacturing sector, without diversification of its economy, Western Canada will be disproportionately affected when the current booming commodity markets flatten. (2009)

Evidence of this reality is seen by the impact of falling potash prices on Saskatchewan's economy in 2009, the collapse of softwood lumber markets and prices when the American housing bubble burst in 2009, and the endemic effect of volatile oil prices on Alberta's economy.

For decades, the federal government has taken a regional approach to economic development (see Dupuis 2011 for an expanded history). As Donald Savoie describes, the federal government has "introduced a veritable alphabet soup of regional development programs and agencies since the 1960s" (2003, 176). As it now stands, all parts of Canada have their own regional development agency: western Canada (WD), northern Ontario (FedNor), Quebec (CED-Q), Atlantic Canada (ACOA), and the North (CanNor). Even southern Ontario, Canada's industrial heartland, now has a regional development agency (FedDev Ontario). The continuation of federal economic development agencies is notable, given that many have questioned the effectiveness and appropriateness of such agencies. Savoie writes:

> It is not too much of an exaggeration to suggest that the federal government has lost its way in the regional development field. It is no longer clear what it wishes to accomplish—it has not resolved the needs versus the opportunities debate and it has not of late been able to establish regional development as something different than a transfer of federal funds in support of provincial government initiatives. Regional development policy now has a serious credibility problem both in the national press and in Ottawa. . . . In any event, every region, strong or weak, has had its hand in the federal regional development pot. However ridiculous it may appear to some, we have reached the point where federal regional development programs in Atlantic Canada can no longer compete with similar federal government programs in other provinces, notably Ontario and Quebec. (2003, 172)

The various regional agencies of the federal government have quite different mandates and budgets. ACOA's mandate, for example, is very broad: to promote economic development in Atlantic Canada "in order to increase the number of jobs and earned income of Atlantic Canadians" (Canada 2012b). The mandate of Western Economic Diversification (WD), as its name would suggest, specifically refers to *diversification* as a policy goal: "to promote the development and diversification of the economy of Western Canada and to advance the interests of the West in national economy policy" (Western Economic Diversification Canada 2012). Thus, for many years WD provided the federal government with a strategic policy window on the West, a function that may be less necessary under present circumstances, and served as the lead agency for federal government disaster relief and engagement with urban policy issues in the region. Given the under-representation of the West in successive Liberal governments of the past, but keeping in mind that WD was brought in by the Progressive Conservative government of Brian Mulroney, the need for a federal agency and voice within the West, and for the West in Ottawa, made sense at the time of its creation in 1986.

Over the last 25 years, however, the diversification mandate of WD has become increasingly elusive and opaque. Initially, the objective was pretty clear-cut: to wean provincial economies off their dependency on natural resource exports and to facilitate the transition to something along the lines of the manufacturing economy in Ontario, which in effect became the national model for those wishing to abandon hewing wood and drawing water. Today, the Ontario model has been hit hard by ever-increasing global competition and an uncertain economic relationship with the United States, and may therefore no longer be the optimal

model for Ontario much less for other regions. At the same time, the
hewers and drawers in western Canada have been doing very well in the
wake of strong global demand for the commodities found in such abundance across the region. These changing economic circumstances have
raised a number of difficult questions:

- If Ontario is no longer the optimal national model, can one be found
  elsewhere? Can we even find a truly *national* model for the regionally
  diverse Canadian economy?
- Should western Canadian provinces try to diversify around the resource
  cores of their provincial economies (e.g., engineering, environmental,
  financial, and project management services) or away from those cores
  (e.g., tourism, video game design, medical research)?
- Should the emphasis be on the diversification of *markets,* such as finding Asian outlets for oil and gas, or on the diversification of *products,*
  moving away from such a heavy reliance on resource exports?
- Does economic diversification entail moving up the value chain,
  exporting petroleum products rather than bitumen, furniture rather
  than logs? And, if this is the case, how do we move up the value chain
  when our markets are determined to keep value-added jobs in their
  own economies?

More fundamentally, should western Canada try to move away from a
resource economy when this may be the region's and perhaps the country's best niche in the global economy? And, if the answer is yes, and
we stress *if*, do we have the policy tools needed for this transformation? Will they be effective if global demand for resource commodities
remains strong while global interest in Canadian value-added products
remains at best indifferent?

One of the drivers for economic diversification has been the assumed
inevitability of resource depletion; what will we do when oil and gas
reserves run dry, when the forests have been cut, and the mines exhausted?
What economic future will we leave to our children and grandchildren?
Yet as critical as these questions are, the more immediate concern is
that markets may dry up faster than reserves in the face of technological change, environmental opposition, slumping consumer demand, and
growing resource production in our traditional export markets. Here we
would note recent predictions that by 2020 the United States may be the
world's largest oil and gas producer. Unfortunately, troubling questions
persist even if markets remain strong, prices remain high, and access
challenges with respect to Asian and American markets are resolved.
Will the western Canadian provincial economies provide a full range

of employment opportunities given that high commodity prices tend to drive out economic diversification—what non-resource-based industry would want to compete with the oil sands for workers and office space in Alberta? Will young people see the need to "go down the road" if their employment interests reach beyond the resource sector? Given the capital-intensive nature of resource production, will the West be able to sustain population growth?

All of these diversification questions apply with equal force to provincial governments, their policy visions, and their policy tools. The challenge here, as for the federal government, is to reduce disincentives to diversification and to create incentives. This is not to say that governments should start to pick "winners" and "losers," prop up non-viable industries, or become major actors in the economy. Far from it, but at the same time public policy has a role to play. Diversification is not an inevitable product of a market-based economy operating in a regional context. Simply put, but not so simple to apply, there is a need to develop strategies to help build the new economy, a knowledge-based economy, in the western provinces. This will mean, in part, building on existing strengths and the existing resource base by developing, for example, petroleum consulting businesses that can compete across the world long after Alberta's conventional oil and natural gas resources are in decline. It may also mean building an agricultural bio-tech industry in Saskatchewan and Manitoba that is immune to seasonal variations in crops, and a multimedia industry in British Columbia that can compete with the world's best (and with the heavily subsidized sector in Quebec).

While advances have been made on these fronts, the opportunities for adding value to natural resource extraction rather than exporting raw materials to be processed elsewhere have not been fully tapped. The West also has an opportunity to expand its "new economy" industries in such fields as biotechnology, medical research, aerospace, and alternative energy sources. Making this transition will require a globally competitive region, defined by a positive business environment (in terms of regulation and tax rates); a high quality of life; and a large, diversified, and skilled labour force. This in turn means that public policy choices will shape the conditions for regional competitiveness and economic diversification. The ideological dilemma is that policy intervention is based on the premise, and we believe the correct premise, that market mechanisms alone will not encourage diversification, that government intervention in the economy is unavoidable if diversification goals are to be achieved. Whether western Canadian electorates will support intervention of sufficient magnitude is by no means certain.

The Political Implications of the Western Economy

The western Canadian provinces share many economic interests, including the need for efficient transportation systems and access to international markets, and their primary exports are subject to often dramatic price volatility. These economic circumstances contribute to specific provincial and at times regional perspectives on national economic policies. Given their constitutional responsibilities for many important economic policy areas, provincial governments—in western Canada and in other regions—are cautious about "national" efforts that may impinge upon provincial economic interests or autonomy; Béland and Lecours argue that "provincial autonomy" has been a driving principle of Canadian federalism since Confederation (2011). Such sensitivities are particularly charged in western Canada for, as discussed in chapter 1, western Canadians—and particularly prairie residents—have come to believe that myriad economic policies from the 1879 National Policy to the 1980 National Energy Program were regionally biased to advantage central Canadian interests at the expense of the West. While one may be tempted to dismiss this history as "all in the past" (after all, the National Policy was a very long time ago), history matters deeply in Canadian politics and this is no less true in the West. These historical economic grievances contributed to a broad-based and highly resilient sentiment that western Canada (and particularly the prairie West) is economically exploited by the rest of Canada.

This sentiment—at times underlying, and at times front and centre—remains highly relevant to national political discourse. While provincial policy will play a key role in determining the future of the western Canadian provincial economies, there is also no doubt as to the real and potential relevancy of federal actions or inaction. Federal disengagement from policy issues driving regional prosperity is impossible unless Ottawa closes its doors. For this reason, economic issues and policies will undoubtedly spill over into national political discussions, for better or for worse. Here we will briefly note three potentially inflammatory issues or sets of issues: environmental protection and climate change, market access, and federal transfers.

Environmental Protection and Climate Change
It is inevitable that resource extraction industries in western Canada will run up against concerns about environmental protection. Such concerns may be specific to the extraction site, directed to the transportation of extracted resources (roads and rail systems, pipelines, electricity transmission lines, ports), or linked to more international concerns

about Canadian contributions to addressing climate change and global warming. Although Alberta's oil sands (or "tar sands," in the vernacular of critics) provide the exemplar for all of these concerns, virtually any resource development will have an environmental footprint. Mines, forestry, and hydro developments are by no means exempt, nor are tourist developments, feedlots, and recreational sites such as ski hills. Although the size and depth of that footprint are diminishing over time as resource companies and others improve their environmental performance, the footprint will never disappear, and may never diminish to the point where the local, regional, national, and international environmental communities will all be satisfied. For some and perhaps many in the environmental movement, local environmental impacts are of secondary concern to the larger struggle against global warming. For example, the community group Voters Taking Action on Climate Change has been protesting new coal mines in southeastern British Columbia; the concerns they express include not only water pollution, but also the contribution of the coal's ultimate consumption, not in Canada but in Asia, to global warming (Hume 2013). More production would require additional port capacity, and any such expansion is being fought by environmental organizations in Vancouver who are concerned about "the role Canada's greenest city is playing in global climate change" (Hume 2013). The sobering lesson here is that resource companies are likely to encounter environmental opposition even if their site-specific environmental impact is reduced to the vanishing point.

Thus, many western Canadian economic interests will remain in the environmental crosshairs for the foreseeable future. And, given concurrent federal and provincial responsibilities with respect to environmental protection, both orders of government will be involved, as will many First Nation governments and local authorities. While governments may take steps to work together (such as the 2012 Joint Canada–Alberta Implementation Plan for Oil Sands Monitoring), there is a huge potential for jurisdictional friction and perhaps conflict. Nothing will be simple about ensuring that resource development in western Canada maintains the social licence to operate—the requisite degree of community consultation and support—it will need.

None of this is to suggest an irreconcilable tension between economic development and environmental protection, although their reconciliation will not be easy. For example, climate change policies, especially if they entail federal initiatives to price carbon, need not be explosive as it all depends on the design of carbon policies. Here there is an important difference between universal programs, albeit ones that might have differential regional effects,[7] and national programs that target particular regions or regionally concentrated industries. Would a carbon tax, for instance, focus on extractive industries, largely although not entirely located in western Canada, or would it apply to all forms of carbon consumption including commuter traffic on Highway 401 in Toronto? What impact might a carbon tax have on the international competitiveness of the regional economy? How much revenue would be raised by any carbon tax, how would that revenue be spent, and by whom? At issue, therefore, is less the imposition of a tax and more the regional distribution of both the tax load and the expenditures that new tax revenues might enable. A carbon tax would not necessarily fall particularly heavily on the West, but a poorly designed tax certainly could.

Part of the backdrop to all of these issues is an emerging debate about the value or desirability of growth itself. In many ways economic growth has been a western Canadian, and for that matter Canadian mantra. Certainly throughout this work we discuss challenges to economic growth, and public policies aimed at promoting growth. Today, discussions of growth are generally prefaced with the adjective "sustainable": few people promote growth that could only be sustained through environmental damage. Others, however, have begun to question the value of growth itself, and have argued that a society preoccupied with growth is encouraging its own demise; "sustainable growth" is dismissed as an oxymoron. While this opposition to the very notion and desirability of economic growth is far from a mainstream orientation, it has begun to shade ideological thought across the country.

Market Access

As noted above, western Canada's huge resource endowment is only so much stuff in the ground unless markets can be found and accessed. When potential markets are international rather than local, it will become increasingly difficult for individual firms to secure market access without a supportive policy environment and, in some cases, even direct public support. Take, for example, the still hypothetical Asian markets for western Canadian natural gas. Any exports will have to move across countless rivers and streams, through wildlife areas and Aboriginal land, out through yet to be built ports, and into complex Asian markets where access may be shaped by international trade agreements such as the Trans Pacific Partnership. It is difficult to see how this complex market access challenge can be addressed by individual firms or consortiums on their own; governments will inevitably be brought into play, certainly through regulatory responsibilities but potentially in other ways as well, including the negotiation of framework agreements with First Nations. And here again, we are not talking about the engagement of single governments, but all governments ranging from Ottawa to provincial legislatures, First Nation assemblies, and local councils.

Potential liquid natural gas (LNG) developments in British Columbia represent only the tip of a much larger government engagement in market access challenges. As noted above, the movement of coal to Asian markets is as much a political issue as it is an economic issue; questions about whether coal exports will damage Vancouver's environmental reputation or unduly offend the environmental values of its residents cannot be reduced to a profit and loss analysis. The proposed Northern Gateway pipeline that would move bitumen from Alberta to ports on the BC coast has sparked an intense political debate in British Columbia, one in which the federal government and national political parties are increasingly engaged. The debate over American approval for the proposed Keystone XL pipeline that would move Alberta bitumen to refineries on the American Gulf Coast has been shaped only in small part by site-specific environmental concerns; the much larger political contest has been between Canadian producers and governments, on the one hand, and, on the other hand, American environmental organizations who maintain that the pipeline is a symbolic line in the sand that must not be transgressed if the battle to contain global warming is to be successful. The new reality is that a dependence on international markets means increased vulnerability to domestic politics within those markets.

Finally, it should be noted that market access can be linked to the politically contentious issue of foreign direct investment (FDI), a policy and regulatory area where the federal government is the primary player. Resource development in western Canada has been and will continue to be fueled by foreign investment; there is not enough Canadian investment to be found. At issue going forward is whether Canada will be "open for business" to sovereign wealth funds and state-owned enterprises, and whether investment brings in its wake market commitments. Is, for example, Chinese investment in the oil sands based on the implicit assumption that oil sands exports to China will eventually be in the offing? Foreign investment controversies have swirled around forestry, potash, and mining developments (e.g., BHP Biliton's unsuccessful attempt to take over the Potash Corporation of Saskatchewan) and around the oil and gas sector (e.g., CNOOC's purchase of Nexen Energy). Such controversies will undoubtedly continue in the years ahead.

Federal Transfers

With annual federal transfers to provinces and territories amounting to over $50 billion, it is not surprising that there are strong opinions regarding the regional allocation of these transfers. The differing economic circumstances of Canadian provinces have implications for provincial perspectives on federal spending, and in particular for the federal equalization program. As of 2013–14, three of Canada's four "have provinces"—that is, provinces that do not receive equalization payments—are located in western Canada: Alberta, British Columbia, and Saskatchewan. (Newfoundland and Labrador is the fourth.) Western Canadian provincial governments have over the years expressed concerns about the fairness of the equalization formula, although not, it should be stressed, about the larger principle of equalization itself. The tricky part of the "western" critique of equalization is that while Alberta has consistently been a "have" province since the late 1950s, British Columbia and Saskatchewan have moved back and forth over the years between "have" and "have not" status, and Manitoba remains a "have not" province. Moving forward, it is possible that the federal government will seek to address some of the political concerns regarding the perceived fairness of equalization through the use of an arms-length agency (rather than the federal government) to set the equalization formula, a proposal put forward by Béland and Lecours (2012), among others.

Looking beyond the formal equalization program, concerns have been raised about what we might call "generic equalization," the propensity of all federal programs to include at least some elements of equalization, in effect shifting resources from the have to the have not provinces; EI is only the most egregious example. There has been a longstanding popular belief in western Canada—and particularly in Alberta—that quite apart from the eastward tip of the equalization program, federal spending overall is skewed to favour Quebec. In the words of columnist Don Martin, "the conventional and well-deserved western view of Ottawa has always been that of a giant money-laundering operation turning honest tax dollars into Quebec payola" (2002, A3). A good example of this perspective can be seen in a 2001 editorial in the *Calgary Herald*:

> In 1998, Alberta dished out $5.7 billion more than it received; by contrast Quebec swallowed $5.9 billion more than it paid. While Quebecers benefited $797 per person from Confederation, Albertans paid out $1,955 each. As Alberta's have-economy expands, so do the demands of the country. Alberta Treasury calculates that the net loss to Albertans grew to $2,651 per person in 1999, and $2,905 in 2000. Albertans wouldn't begrudge the financial imbalance; helping one's neighbour is a value that thrives in the West. It's just that a little appreciation is long overdue. (2001, OS6)

In the decade since this editorial was published, little has happened to erode the sentiments expressed. We would only add that Albertans are by no means alone in their dissatisfaction; in recent years, the Ontario government and the University of Toronto's Mowat Centre, among others, have also raised concerns about the fairness of federal transfers.

Although the principle of equalization continues to receive broad political and public support in western Canada, the generic application of that principle across the full range of federal programs is much more contentious. As the incumbent Conservative government continues to move toward per capita transfers for federal expenditures falling outside the equalization program per se—the Canadian Health Transfer (CHT) and the Canadian Social Transfer (CST) are the biggest examples—political attention will shift more and more to the negotiations to renew the equalization formula in 2015, negotiations that will be closely watched in western Canada.

Conclusion

We began this chapter with a discussion about the 2012 debate about western Canada's economic interests and their purported negative implications for the national economy. While we certainly do not intend to discuss the merits or faults of the "Dutch disease" argument, we will note that the pitting of regional economies against each other is problematic for national unity. In the days of the Grain Economy there was no question that the regional economy in western Canada was seen as a national asset; it supported a unique regional way of life (Fowke 1957, 282) while also providing a mainstay of the national economy:

> As the annual wheat crop moved from the western farm to the loading ports of the east it served to justify an expensive system of transcontinental railroads, while the proceeds of its sale enabled the farmer in the West both to buy eastern manufactures, which in turn became the westbound traffic on the railroads, and to pay for the financial services offered him by banks, grain traders, and mortgage companies. Almost the whole Canadian economy was vitally affected by, and organized around, the movement of the annual grain crop into world markets. (Mallory 1953, 38)

Thus, a strong regional economy in the West was fully compatible with, indeed indispensable to, national economic strength.

Unfortunately, this perspective may be changing. To go back to the introduction to this chapter, arguments about Dutch disease abandon this logic by arguing that western strength leads to "national" weakness. Some environmentalists make a complementary argument, that western strength based on resource extraction runs contrary to basic Canadian values. These changes are significant for national policy debates. Given the West's growing share of the national population and its growing contribution to the national economy, debates about regional prosperity, debates from the early days of agricultural settlement to the oil sands, have really been debates about national prosperity. What has changed is that the regional components of the national economy are becoming even more loosely connected; the determinants of prosperity in Ontario and the West are not the same, and prosperity in one region no longer necessarily fosters prosperity in other regions.

Although in this chapter we have discussed a number of economic and policy challenges that are particularly acute in western Canada, our regional focus should not leave the impression that these challenges are unique to the West. For example, while labour shortages could severely constrain economic growth in the West, they will also pose a challenge across the country, and thus debates about immigration policy, EI reform, and the engagement of older workers are first national debates, and only secondarily regional debates. Our argument throughout is less that the western Canadian provincial economies are unique, and more that they bring into bold relief *national* challenges and policies. A complementary argument is that recent economic growth in the West is not a short-term blip but rather reflects enduring structural change in the Canadian economy. Therefore if we want to peer ahead into the murky crystal ball of Canada's economic future, we should begin by looking at the West, not because it is unique but because it is in western Canada that our economic future will be shaped, for better or for worse.

Notes

1   The data presented in this chapter are drawn from Roach (2010) and Statistics Canada (2012a, 2012e), unless otherwise noted.

2   The authors would like to thank Robert Roach from the Canada West Foundation for providing these figures.

3   Section 36.2 of the 1982 *Constitution Act* states that "Parliament and the government of Canada are committed to the principle of making equalization payments to ensure that provincial governments have sufficient revenues to provide reasonably comparable levels of public services at reasonably comparable levels of taxation."

4   To structure our discussion, we found it useful to draw on the results of the Canada West Foundation's 2011 Honourable James A. Richardson Discovery

Roundtables. These roundtables, held in Vancouver, Edmonton, Regina, and Winnipeg, brought together stakeholders to discuss the economic future of western Canada. The key themes raised at the roundtables were: creating the conditions for growth, opening new markets, ensuring the availability of high quality labour, and fostering innovation and entrepreneurship (see Holden 2012). We have adapted these themes to frame our discussion.

5   Although the federal government cannot legislate in provincial areas of jurisdiction, the courts have not imposed any constitutional limitations on federal *spending* in provincial areas of jurisdiction. When such spending is tied to conditions that provincial and territorial governments must meet, the federal government has very real leverage on provincial programming and policy priorities.

6   The four western provinces vary in the specific character of their export resource dependency: wood, fibre, coal, and potentially natural gas in British Columbia; oil, natural gas, and agricultural products in Alberta; agricultural products, oil and gas, potash and uranium in Saskatchewan. Only Manitoba has a diversified export profile that features a greater reliance on manufactured products.

7   Old Age Security payments are the same regardless of where seniors might happen to live. However, if the proportion of seniors is greater in one province than another, then the national program will provide unequal regional benefits.

4.   Considerations on the West as a Political Region

IN APRIL 2010, Canada's three westernmost provinces, British Columbia, Alberta, and Saskatchewan, announced the New West Partnership. This agreement laid out intentions for the three provinces to adopt a regional approach across a number of policy areas, and the future for regional collaboration and cooperation in western Canada (albeit a "West" without Manitoba) seemed bright. Indeed, the signing premiers proclaimed that this intergovernmental cooperation agreement meant that "[w]ith one voice, the West will be a leader on issues that are vital to the nation's competitiveness. . . . The New West Partnership will help Saskatchewan, Alberta and British Columbia become stronger both as provinces, as a regional power in Canada and abroad" (Wall, Stelmach, and Campbell 2010).

Jump forward two years. By spring 2012, two of the three signing premiers, Gordon Campbell (British Columbia) and Ed Stelmach (Alberta), had retired from electoral politics; only Brad Wall (Saskatchewan) remained. Although Alberta's new premier, Alison Redford, showed no sign of abandoning a regional approach, her primary objective appeared to be to assert Alberta's leadership on the national stage, particularly with respect to advocacy for a Canadian Energy Strategy. Christy Clark was the new premier of British Columbia and, facing the potential electoral defeat of her Liberal government, seemed to be stepping away from regional approaches in favour of a more BC-centric approach. She skipped the May 2012 Western Premiers' Conference, and in August provoked a high-profile confrontation with Premier Redford over the proposed Northern Gateway Pipeline project. While the New West

Partnership remains intact—in September 2012, the three premiers co-hosted a New West Partnership reception in Tianjin, China, as part of the World Economic Forum—BC's long-term commitment to the partnership, and to regional approaches more broadly, is uncertain. And still, Manitoba stands apart.

In this book, we have consistently viewed western Canada through a regional lens. In doing so, we have built on a long tradition of scholarship, not to mention political debate and media discussion, that stresses the political relevance of regions and regionalism in Canada (see, for example, Bell 1992; Blake 1972; Brodie 1990; Elkins and Simeon 1980; Gibbins 1982; Gidengil et al. 1999; Ornstein, Stevenson, and Williams 1980; Savoie 2000; Simeon and Elkins 1974). At differing times and in differing ways, "regions" matter to intergovernmental relations, institutional representation, voting patterns, and public attitudes. The challenge in adopting a regional lens, however, is that regional definitions vary considerably, depending on context: the eastern provinces are at different times referred to as "Atlantic Canada" (all four easternmost provinces) and "the Maritimes" (Nova Scotia, New Brunswick, and Prince Edward Island, with Newfoundland and Labrador treated as distinct); Ontario and Quebec are still occasionally, although not frequently, bundled together as "central Canada"; and the three territories are often grouped simply as "the North." In western Canada, one hears of either "the Prairies" (Alberta, Saskatchewan, and Manitoba, with British Columbia treated as distinct) or "the West," which typically includes all four western provinces (the conceptual definition adopted for this book) but has recently been redefined by provincial governments as British Columbia, Alberta, and Saskatchewan in the New West Partnership agreement. The current federal government has its own unique approach, referring in the singular to the "Prairie and Pacific Region."

There can be no doubt that the notion of "western Canada," its reality on the ground, is contentious for some and perhaps many. Victoria residents waiting in line at the latest trendy food truck may bristle at the idea that they can somehow be lumped together with residents of Red Deer, Moose Jaw, Flin Flon, or even Vancouver! Scholars, including ourselves (Gibbins and Berdahl 2003), may note the "east-west divide" within western Canada, with important differences between the more populous "western western" provinces and the less populous "eastern western" provinces. The four western Canadian provincial governments' interest in regional approaches varies with premiers' personalities and political circumstances, and the federal government adopts a regional model for some policy issues (economic development in particular), a province-by-province model for others, and a national model for still other areas.

In our opinion, there is no point in arguing that western Canada is (or is not) a region by some clear, universally agreed upon understanding of "region." It is our position that the definition of regions is fluid and situational. Political scientist Philip Resnick captures this reality when he writes, "For certain purposes, BC's inhabitants and politicians feel themselves part of western Canada or the West, yet for others they feel themselves apart from the other western provinces, including Alberta" (2000, 19). At times—in certain political circumstances, in particular contexts—a regional lens or approach makes sense; at other times, it does not. To paraphrase former prime minister William Lyon Mackenzie King's comment on conscription during World War II, the West is a region if necessary but not necessarily a region.

Thus, trying to impose a "western Canadian" label that applies in all circumstances is foolhardy. Whether the four western provinces should be treated as a region, at least in some respects and circumstances, is an open question, and the answer all depends on the criteria we use. Certainly there is little constitutional expression of regionalism, although the West is a Senate region unlike the others in its allocation of seats. In the chapters thus far, we have noted how the four western provinces have a number of shared characteristics; specifically, we have presented evidence that the four western provinces share a number of demographic (chapter 2) and economic (chapter 3) commonalities, and have suggested that there is a distinctive regional political culture, one with deep historical roots and considerable geographic reach (chapter 1). However, we have not yet demonstrated that provincial governments in the West *act* regionally—that is, adopt regional approaches to provincial policy challenges, present regional positions in national political debates and act as a "united front" with respect to federal policy. Nor, for that matter, have we demonstrated that residents of the four provinces "think" regionally, or consider themselves in some meaningful way as part of a regional community.

To explore these issues, we begin this chapter by outlining both the case for and the very real impediments to (and limitations of) regional approaches. We move to outline the current state of regional cooperation in western Canada, directing particular attention to the institutional structures that might support a regional model. Finally, we explore the extent to which regional strategies, were they to be pursued further in the future, would build on an underlying "region of the mind."[1] Over the course of the chapter, we demonstrate that while a case can be made for advancing regional cooperation, and while evidence exists of some public attitudinal support for "acting" as a region, western Canadian regional approaches to public policy are and will continue to be characterized by limited institutionalization.

Regional Cooperation: Advantages, Limitations, and Impediments

Although Canadian scholars devote considerable attention to federal–provincial–territorial intergovernmental relations (or "FPT relations," in the vernacular of the federalism literature), very little attention is paid to the relationships between and among provincial (and territorial) governments ("PT relations"). This scholarly neglect is curious given the realities of both considerable interprovincial cooperation (for examples, see Leach 1959; Pelletier 2002, 28; Fox and Roach 2003) and the increasing frequency of PT interactions over time (Simmons 2004; Berdahl 2011).

There are a number of reasons why provincial and territorial governments choose to cooperate on public policy and other matters. One is that interprovincial cooperation can be used to deal with "spillover" issues without engaging the federal government. Governments face a slew of policy issues that cannot be bottled up within provincial boundaries. Transportation connections to the global economy, for example, do not start and end at provincial boundaries; even the Port of Vancouver, perched on the edge of the Pacific Ocean, is not only a regional terminus but also the terminus for a national transportation system that snakes for thousands of kilometres back into the interior of the continent. Environmental effects are oblivious to political lines on the map, and common waterways cross multiple provinces. Individuals may go to school in one province, work in another, and perhaps retire in yet another, only incidentally aligning public services with where taxes are paid. In effect, there is a great deal of spillover across provincial and jurisdictional boundaries, aided and abetted by a good deal of individual mobility.

One possible approach to handling such spillovers is to assign legislative responsibility for issues that cross provincial boundaries to the national government. For example, Ottawa could pick up responsibility for many transportation systems, given that road and rail links do not end at provincial boundaries, and for manpower training (including post-secondary education) given the mobility of the Canadian labour force. In a similar fashion, responsibility for environmental protection could be lodged with the national government. This approach, however, would result in a massive migration of powers and responsibilities to

Ottawa, perhaps to the extent of eliminating federalism as a meaningful concept in Canada. Not surprisingly, this solution enjoys no support from provincial governments and very little public support except when such a transfer might benefit a particular policy interest or agenda, including the potential infusion of federal funding. From the perspective of most governments—indeed, even the Government of Canada in most cases—cooperation among provincial governments is a far more attractive alternative.

Economies of scale provide another rationale for interprovincial cooperation. With a small population spread over a large and imposing landmass, provinces may sometimes find that there are economic advantages to joint programs and joint procurement. For example, provinces could work together to jointly fund and administer international offices (such as the New West Partnership's Shanghai trade office, established in 2010), and groups of provinces may be able to secure more favourable pharmaceutical drug procurements when working together, purchasing on behalf of larger populations (such as the generic price setting initiative announced by the Council of the Federation in 2012). Generally speaking, then, interprovincial cooperation may be pursued at either a subnational or pan-Canadian level with the goals of improved program efficiencies and more cost-effective government.

Interprovincial cooperation can also be an important political tool in federal–provincial relations. It is often said the federal government takes a "divide and conquer" approach to the provinces, pitting some provinces against others to weaken the collective voice of the provincial governments. Interprovincial cooperation can help provinces and territories present a "united front" in federal–provincial relations, and thus communiqués from PT meetings regularly include a list of demands for federal action or policy direction. The effectiveness of this strategy in Canada has been limited since the 1990s due to the fact that prime ministers have largely been unwilling to meet with premiers multilaterally, instead preferring to meet with premiers individually.

While interprovincial cooperation has its advantages—policy coordination without federal intervention, potential program efficiencies, and a strengthened provincial position in both federal–provincial relations and international trade promotion—there are also important constraints.[2] One is the reality that provinces are in many ways competitors (Zimmerman 1996). Alberta and Saskatchewan, for example, use royalty systems to compete for oil and gas investment, just as British Columbia and Alberta compete for gas investment in the rich fields spanning northwestern Alberta and northeastern British Columbia. Provincial governments are actively trying to attract interprovincial migrants, immigrants, and business investment in what is often a zero-sum environment.[3] Provincial governments have a mandate to protect and promote the economic well-being of their specific province, and limited incentives to protect or promote the economic interests of other provinces, even within a regional framework. This competition can be seen as a national advantage to the extent that it promotes policy innovation and creativity, but it also limits the motivations for interprovincial cooperation.

Cooperation may be impeded if provinces attempt to export policy problems to other jurisdictions (Beyle 1974). An example of this was seen under Alberta Premier Ralph Klein:

> When Ralph Klein came to power in 1992, he stopped at nothing to fulfill his promise to fix Alberta's deficit. Infamously, he offered free one-way bus tickets to welfare recipients if they would leave the province. Some took him up on the deal, to the annoyance of politicians in Ontario and British Columbia, who had their own financial problems to worry about. Klein didn't care. His province came first, and voters loved him for it. (Decloet 2012)

Scholars argue that intergovernmental cooperation requires a foundation of "trust ties" (Dupré 1988; Cameron and Simeon 2002, 65), and actions such as Premier Klein's must certainly erode interprovincial relationships. A more contemporary example of exported policy problems is the proposed Northern Gateway Pipeline. Although the project does not directly involve governments, BC Premier Clark argued that Alberta will get the financial gains from Gateway—royalties from bitumen production—while British Columbia will carry the costs of the environmental risks. To paraphrase the well-known country and western song, "Alberta gets the gold mine and British Columbia gets the shaft."

The challenge of too many actors can also impede interprovincial cooperation, particularly at the pan-Canadian level. While there are many examples of pan-Canadian cooperation efforts,[4] interprovincial cooperation *agreements* often involve only a handful of provinces and territories, and the parties are typically geographically concentrated. The tendency toward bilateral and multilateral, as opposed to pan-Canadian, interprovincial cooperation makes sense; pan-Canadian efforts are often "unlikely or unmanageable because of the size and diversity of the Canadian federation" (Roach 2003, 7), whereas geographically connected provinces enjoy the advantages of fewer actors and (potentially) shared policy interests due to common economic and demographic conditions (Meekison 2004b; Roach 2003; Zimmerman 2002).

But although the challenges of interprovincial competition and the management of numerous actors with unique interests are important impediments to interprovincial cooperation, perhaps the greatest limitation is the unwillingness of provinces to cede autonomy to meaningful institutional structures that would facilitate cooperation. Writing about the American context, Zimmerman argues that states have a "natural reluctance" to cooperate due to the "loss of exclusive control" (1996, 213). Such reluctance to transfer autonomy to another body (such as a regional institution, a binding arbitration board, or the judiciary) is also present in Canada, and is understandable given a federal system that "encourages both governments and societies to orient on provincial, not regional lines . . . the institutions of federalism interact with social forces to create durable provincialisms, which are resistant to any trans-provincial regionalism" (Finbow 2004, 164, 167).

These "durable provincialisms" make major interprovincial agreements (such as TILMA and the New West Partnership Trade Agreement, discussed below) highly unusual and result in somewhat limited institutional supports for interprovincial cooperation. One can imagine a continuum of interprovincial cooperation. At the one end of the continuum, cooperation is highly ad hoc: provinces cooperate on a case-by-case basis, lacking mechanisms (such as regular meetings and/or formal institutions) for regular communication. At the other end of the continuum lies regional integration, defined as "greater cooperation among provinces through policy harmonization, new forms of association, and communication across provincial boundaries" (Tomblin 1995, 3). Each approach has its advantages and disadvantages. Ad hoc approaches protect provincial autonomy and allow for maximum flexibility to meet province-specific needs (Bolleyer 2006). Furthermore, ad hoc approaches *can* be effective: in her analysis of ministerial conferences, Simmons (2004) finds that successful outcomes are a result of political will, personalities and external pressures, rather than of formalization and institutionalization. At the same time, ad hoc approaches mean that interprovincial cooperation efforts can be easily stalled or abandoned, and are highly vulnerable to changes in political leadership.

More institutionalized approaches, for their part, can increase the potential for successful policy coordination: "Institutionalization and integration shape whether and how effectively governments can deal with coordination pressures . . . high institutionalization favours the drafting of precise and substantial agreements" (Bolleyer 2009, 8–9). In more colloquial terms, institutionalized models push governments to move beyond talking like regional ducks to actually walking like regional ducks. The risk with this is that the presence of institutions may at times propel parties to cooperate when cooperation is neither necessary nor desirable (Scharpf 1988), in effect "substitut[ing] process for purpose or means for the ends, reducing public policy to the lowest common denominator" (Careless 1989, 33; Simeon 2001 makes a similar critique). Cooperation for its own sake is a dubious goal; while there can be benefits to cooperation, interprovincial collaboration is a means to an end, and not a goal in and of itself. As Emery and Kneebone argue, collaboration can have economic benefits in specific cases, but "there is little hard evidence to justify a blanket statement advocating policy coordination over all tax categories and all spending programs" (2003, 16).

The challenge, then, is to find a balance between excessive ad hockery, where ineffective institutional structures result in insufficient collaboration, and institutional structures that promote unnecessary levels of cooperation. Striking this balance may be more pertinent now than in the past; indeed, some argue that regional cooperation is more necessary in the face of changing global realities and growing global competition. If it is true that globalization creates growing incentives for regional cooperation, ad hoc approaches to cooperation may be inadequate for contemporary realities.

Having outlined the general theoretical case for and limitations of regional cooperation, we shall return our attention to the specific case of western Canada. Here, two questions demand attention: first, what is the current state of interprovincial cooperation; and second, what is the potential for increased interprovincial cooperation moving forward? Or, to return to the "duck" analogy, to what extent are the western provinces walking like regional ducks, and to what extent is there further opportunity to do so?

Regional Models in Western Canada: More Talk than Walk?

We began this chapter with a discussion of the New West Partnership (NWP). A number of things are notable about that agreement. First, and most obviously, the agreement does not include Manitoba—an exclusion that speaks to the rather fluid nature with which "regions" in Canada are defined, and to the importance of ideological relationships in defining and constructing regional agreements and bodies. Second, and looking more deeply into the partnership, three of the four agreements contained within it are voluntary, allowing participating provinces to opt in or out as they see fit, without penalty or consequence; only the interprovincial trade agreement is binding on the signatory provinces. Finally, the NWP does not go so far as to create any form of political integration among the participating provinces. While pursuing greater economic integration and policy harmonization, the three provinces were careful not to relinquish any political autonomy; they did not establish new institutional bodies, or even an institutional structure, such as a secretariat, to coordinate their meetings.

In many ways, the New West Partnership agreement reflects long-standing themes of western Canadian regional approaches: shifting regional configurations, voluntary agreements, and limited institutionalization. In this section, we explore western regional cooperation in greater detail, and in particular the extent to which it has been institutionalized. In doing so, we suggest that the lack of institutional structures to support western Canadian cooperation means that regional cooperation is dependent on the political will of individual premiers.

Western Premiers' Conference

Regional cooperation in Canada finds its early institutional roots in the east, not the west. In 1953, the Atlantic premiers met with business leaders to discuss regional cooperation; shortly thereafter, the premiers created the non-governmental Atlantic Provinces Economic Council (APEC), a body that exists to this day, "to survey, study, stimulate, and coordinate activities relating to the economic well-being of the Atlantic provinces" (Conrad 1993, 405). In 1956, under pressure from Prime Minister St. Laurent to adopt regional approaches to common challenges (Tomblin 1995, 81), the Atlantic premiers began what became annual meetings, and in the early 1960s, New Brunswick Premier Louis Robichaud took an active role in promoting Atlantic regional cooperation, going so far as to discuss regional union (Stanley 1993, 424). While Newfoundland ceased participating in the Atlantic premiers' conferences after 1965, the three maritime premiers appointed the Maritime Union Study (the "Deutsch Commission") to consider expanding regional integration (Stanley 1993, 424), and the 1970 Maritime Union Report called for the eventual union of the three provinces. However, by the time of its release, two of the study's three initiating premiers were gone and the new premiers had limited enthusiasm for full integration (Tomblin 1995, 93). Instead, the premiers opted to formalize their annual meetings into the Council of Maritime Premiers (CMP), established in 1971. In 2000, the CMP was expanded to include Newfoundland and Labrador and renamed the Council of Atlantic Premiers (CAP).

Atlantic regional cooperation is unique in Canada in that its institutional structures are "exceptionally highly developed and not representative of the overall level of institutionalization in Canada" (Bolleyer 2009, 186). As Dennison explains,

The Council's record of endurance and achievement may be
attributed in part to its strong institutional base. . . . It follows a
regular meeting pattern, rotating the Chairmanship and location
with each meeting, and has a permanent secretariat serving
the Council and its agencies, with a total of 28 employees. . . .
The Council operates under a proactive mandate, promoting
regional cooperation generally, and economic cooperation specifically. These mandates are not only spelled out in agreements
but are actually legislated, through mirror legislation in each
jurisdiction. . . . There is no other example in Canada of intergovernmental cooperation and coordination that features a common legislative base, integrated institutions, common employees
supported by an intergovernmental secretariat, and a history
spanning almost 35 years. (2005, 7–8)

The effects of such institutionalization are clear: "This established
base has enabled the Council to be sustained through varying levels of
collective enthusiasm, changes in political and bureaucratic leadership,
and expansion to include Newfoundland and Labrador, with whom
regional ties and common identities are weaker" (Dennison 2005, 7).
Institutionalization does not necessarily result in significant policy
outcomes—efforts to advance a regional model in Atlantic Canada
have been hindered at times by socio-economic disparities between
and within the provinces, competition between the provinces, and debates
about "the very concept of an Atlantic region" (Reid 1993, 473)—but
the very presence of institutional structures promotes longevity.

Western Canadian regional cooperation also has an institutional
home, but the level of institutionalization is much less formalized. Formal
cooperation began in 1965 when the three prairie premiers formed the
Prairie Economic Council, an annual premiers' meeting focused on economic policy coordination. When British Columbia joined in 1973, the
group was renamed the Western Economic Council (Thorburn 1984,
121) and, after the 1973 Western Economic Opportunities Conference
(WEOC), the group evolved into the Western Premiers' Conference
(WPC) (Meekison 2004a, 185). In 1992, the Yukon and the Northwest
Territories began to participate in the WPC, and after Nunavut was created in 1999, it too joined the WPC, which is now an annual event
preceded by a fair degree of intergovernmental consultation. At the
same time, the WPC itself has only weak institutional ties (Bolleyer
2009, 79). Case in point, there is no regional organization that supports the WPC. Instead, "[t]he host province acts as the conference coor-
dinator and provides the secretariat services. The premier of the host

province or territory acts as the spokesperson of the group" (Meekison 2004a, 191).

To what extent does the WPC result in regional approaches to policy or federal provincial relations? The WPC has certainly allowed the western provinces to take a regional approach toward the federal government. The premiers' meetings have provided a way to amplify the West's regional voice, as a group of premiers speaking in unison carries more weight with Ottawa (and other premiers, for that matter) than do individual governments speaking alone. This strategy has been particularly useful in past constitutional debates. Further, Meekison asserts, "the WPC has been instrumental in causing the federal government to change some of its policies," and argues that WPC positions on fiscal federalism "are not easily shrugged off by the federal government" (2004a, 203). The WPC may also influence interprovincial/territorial relations and policy reaching beyond the West. Prior to the 2003 establishment of the Council of the Federation (COF), premiers would meet annually in the late summer at the Annual Premiers' Conference (APC); COF now meets annually in the summer and often in the winter as well. Meekison (2004a) argues that by deliberately holding the WPC meetings in the spring, the western premiers were able to influence the agenda and outcomes of the APCs; the prominence of the Canadian Energy Strategy at COF's 2012 meeting suggests that the WPC continues to influence the national interprovincial/territorial agenda.

While the WPC may result in regional position-taking regarding the federal government and national policy debates, the WPC has not resulted in regional programs or policy initiatives jointly administered and funded by the four western provincial governments. Although a few innovative steps have been taken, including the joint funding of the veterinary program at the University of Saskatchewan, interprovincial policy emerging directly from the WPC is very limited. WPC communiqués provide a useful itemization of regional grievances with respect to Ottawa, but offer much thinner gruel with respect to common action on the part of the provincial governments. The WPC's essential role is political rather than administrative or governmental. It serves to strengthen personal relationships among the premiers and territorial leaders, and many of its activities are directed to this end. Those personal relationships can in turn provide the foundation upon which more institutionalized relationships might be built, but to this point construction activity has been modest.

The WPC also has a design feature that may complicate or even preclude significant evolution toward regional governance. As noted earlier, since the early 1990s, the WPC has brought together not only the premiers of British Columbia, Alberta, Saskatchewan, and Manitoba, but also the territorial leaders of the Yukon and the Northwest Territories; after the creation of Nunavut, its premier joined as well. Thus, the WPC conflates two regions, the West and the North, into a single intergovernmental vehicle, and the territories with their considerably smaller population base, much greater dependence on federal funding, and ongoing campaign for greater control and ownership with respect to natural resources (a battle that has been largely fought and won in the provincial West), have some unique interests setting them apart from the western provinces. This is not to say that the territorial leaders have stood in the way of the western premiers discussing western-specific matters at the WPC. At the same time, it is notable that while there has been a separate annual Northern Premiers' Forum since 2003,[5] there is not yet a separate annual meeting of the four western premiers.

Overall, the WPC is considerably less institutionalized than is the APC. This is not necessarily a problem, and may simply reflect that regional cooperation in western Canada is arguably more complex than in Atlantic Canada: the larger physical expanse of the western region, and the greater economic and demographic diversities among the western provinces, render the regional threads more delicate in the West than in the East. As such, the flexibility of the WPC's regional model may well be a strength, rather than a weakness, as it allows the premiers to build relationships that can be expanded into other, more policy-focused, cooperation efforts, such as is seen with the New West Partnership.

New West Partnership

The New West Partnership (NWP) Agreement, signed by the premiers of British Columbia, Alberta, and Saskatchewan in 2010, seeks to create (in the provinces' words) a "seamless economic region." Of course, "seamless economic regions" do not simply emerge without some preparation work. The New West Partnership is the outcome of over seven years of effort to create, develop, and market a strong western Canadian "economic region." British Columbia and Alberta began working together in 2003: on June 11, 2003, the two provinces signed a cooperation agreement, and on October 8, 2003, they held a joint cabinet meeting. Annual BC–Alberta joint cabinet meetings, and a large number of interprovincial agreements, including the Trade, Investment, and Labour Mobility Agreement (TILMA, discussed further below), followed until 2008. On September 9, 2008, less than a year after the election of the Saskatchewan Party government, Alberta and Saskatchewan held a joint cabinet meeting. In 2009, the three westernmost provinces shifted to trilateral joint cabinet meetings, with meetings held in March 2009, September 2009, and April 2010. It was at the April 2010 meeting that the NWP was signed (Berdahl 2011).

The NWP is an umbrella partnership that contains four distinct agreements. The most notable of these is the New West Partnership Trade Agreement (NWPTA), a legally binding agreement designed to reduce non-tariff internal trade barriers among the three signatory provinces. Some background is necessary here. While Canadian provinces have long-voiced a commitment to address non-tariff internal trade barriers, most notably in the 1995 Agreement on Internal Trade (AIT), progress in actually doing so was slow (see Berdahl 2013). In the 2000s, British Columbia and Alberta began to work together to address these barriers on a bilateral basis,[6] with the goal of establishing a liberalized internal trade region within Canada. The expansion of their efforts can be seen in the progression of interprovincial agreements in the 2003–10 period. British Columbia and Alberta signed the Internal Trade Framework Agreement in 2004, which led to the signing of the TILMA in 2006. TILMA sought to establish a two-province economic region by harmonizing business regulation, procurement, subsidies, and occupational standards for professionals and skilled tradespersons. TILMA represented a significant step forward in internal trade policy in that, unlike the AIT with its voluntary compliance approach, it created binding commitments between the signatory governments: provinces risk up to a $5 million penalty if they fail to comply with the terms of the agreement, and must give 12 months written notice to withdraw from the agreement.[7] Saskatchewan joined the region-building process in 2008, and the three westernmost provinces signed the Western Economic Partnership Agreement in 2009, followed by the New West Partnership Trade Agreement (NWPTA), an expansion of TILMA to include Saskatchewan, in 2010.

While internal trade is a central component of the New West Partnership, it is not the entirety of the partnership. The NWP also includes the New West Partnership Procurement Agreement, in which the three provinces state their intention to "work together to jointly purchase goods and services in order to achieve efficiencies and cost-savings"; the New West Partnership Innovation Agreement, in which the three provinces state their intention to pursue joint projects and share information with respect to research and development activities, particularly regarding forestry and carbon capture and storage; and the New West Partnership International Cooperation Agreement, in which the three provinces state their intention to "collaborate on high-quality, cost-effective joint international initiatives" (Alberta, British Columbia, and Saskatchewan 2010a, 2010c, 2010d).

Although it is not yet clear to what extent the three provinces are following through on their stated intentions to cooperate with respect to procurement and innovation, the three signing premiers (Campbell, Stelmach, and Wall) used the New West Partnership as an opportunity for international marketing and branding. In May 2010, just one month after the NWP signing, the three premiers made a joint trade mission to China and Japan, and opened a joint trade and investment office in Shanghai. Statements made by the premiers suggest that they saw potential economic advantages in presenting western Canada as a single region to international audiences. In the words of Alberta Premier Stelmach, "We've just gone through a huge global economic shift. There's going to be a tremendous competition for labour, for investment. And investment will naturally navigate to those areas that have the same regulations, larger base populations" (as quoted in Alberta Federation of Labour, 2010). Saskatchewan Premier Wall spoke explicitly in branding terms:

> We'll have the advantage of promoting Western Canada. Rather than trying to carve out a brand for each individual province, we're going to build on the strength [and] leverage the strength of the Canadian brand, specifically the western Canadian brand. (As quoted in Cernetig 2010, 14)

And BC Premier Campbell stressed the competitive advantages of taking a regional approach: "We're saying we're a unified market, a region of nine million people with a GDP of half-a-trillion dollars. I think it gives us more influence when we're together" (as quoted in Cernetig 2010).

Arguably, the regional integration that is sought through the NWP represents a significant advance in intergovernmental cooperation in Canada, and an important example of western Canadian policy leadership. But while it established a legal framework for more liberalized internal trade among the provinces, launched a joint international trade mission, and at the very least stated intentions for future cooperation regarding procurement and research and development, it did not establish an institutional "home" for western Canada—at least not at the formal "summit" level (such as high profile premiers' meetings or clearly defined institutional structures). That being said, the NWP has resulted in considerable collaboration at the public service level as officials across the three provinces regularly work together to deal with the technicalities of implementing the agreement. Thus, at a functional level, the NWP is considerably more institutionalized than is the WPC, and it has allowed for strengthened day-to-day working relationships among the three provinces.

While NWP policy work has shifted largely to respective provincial departments, in the absence of robust institutional structures the future of the NWP depends very much on the personalities of the sitting premiers and on the political will of their governments. The three provinces could simply choose to not meet, could individually pull out of or jointly agree to close the joint Shanghai office, and could ignore the stated cooperation intentions of the procurement, innovation, and international marketing agreements. Disentanglement from the NWPTA would take longer due to the requirement for 12 months' notice, but would still be possible (although given the ongoing work within the provinces to coordinate standards and practices, dismantling the agreement arguably becomes more difficult with the passage of time). In short, the NWP could be "undone," and both changes in provincial leadership (be it changes in government or simply changes in premier) as well as rifts between premiers—such as the strain between British Columbia and Alberta with respect to proposed pipelines—present true threats to the survival of the NWP. In the face of political conflict, premiers would likely face little electoral risk if they attempted to dismantle the NWP. Intergovernmental cooperation among the western provinces has not been subjected to much public scrutiny, the alignment between intergovernmental agreements and public opinion has yet to be tested, and public interest in intergovernmental relations is low at best.

Yet another limitation to the NWP as a "home" or "voice" for western Canada is the exclusion of Manitoba—a point which becomes visually striking when one considers the partnership's logo, an image of the three participating provinces, with the right side of a maple leaf taking the place of Manitoba. The potential future inclusion of Manitoba in the partnership is uncertain, and the absence of Manitoba raises important questions about the role of the province in the present and future "West." While the Manitoba government has been on record expressing concerns about the internal trade agreement (Goerzen 2010), subsequent media reports suggested that Premier Selinger may have changed his position to become more open to the agreement. Further, while the New Democratic Manitoba government may have lacked sufficient ideological congruence with the three participating provinces at the time of the agreement's signing, this too may have changed, as Alberta Premier Redford is widely acknowledged as being more centrist than her predecessor. These developments will be important to track over time, as the engagement of Manitoba may be a way to breathe new life into the partnership.

Future Interprovincial Cooperation in Western Canada

In the absence of strong regional bodies, regional cooperation in Canada is highly dependent upon the personalities and interests of the sitting premiers. When premiers within a region enjoy a certain interpersonal "chemistry" and share a common vision (or a common "enemy"), regional approaches are more likely to be adopted and advanced. However, these ad hoc partnerships can be tenuous: a change in government in one province, or even a change in leadership, such as the governing party's selection of a new leader and thus new premier, can upset the regional dynamic. As "[e]ssential regional cooperation can progress only so far without political integration" (Finbow 2004, 164), it is perhaps no surprise that "[h]istory is littered with regional visions that never came to pass" (Tomblin 2007, 2).

Should western regional institutionalization be increased? Should the western provinces be pursuing greater regional policy cooperation and coordination? While our discussion of the limits of the existing models implicitly suggest that the answer to both questions is yes, it is important to note that greater institutionalization may undercut opportunities for provincial policy innovation and competition. Further, the flexibility inherent in the current regional models may be better suited to the region's needs than a more formalized approach.

That being said, if some or all of the western provinces wish to pursue greater regional cooperation, what might an alternative model look like? One model, noted earlier, is to establish greater institutionalization along the lines seen in Atlantic Canada. The Council of Atlantic Premiers (CAP) has regular meetings, a permanent secretariat and a mandate for cooperation, and this institutionalization is argued to have contributed to the organization's longevity and, more importantly, to the advancement of regional cooperation. If the western Canadian provinces see true advantages in a more collaborative approach—and we recognize this is a big "if"—then the creation of such an institution would seem the logical next step. Admittedly, the Atlantic provinces had certain advantages in adopting a regional model: in addition to closer geographic proximity, they have had strong external incentives to act, specifically federal pressure, the threat of Quebec separation, and the need to be seen to respond to the 1970 Maritime Union Report discussed earlier. The western provinces face a different situation: in addition to covering a vast landmass (there are 1,900 kilometres between Victoria and Winnipeg), there are no strong external pressures to advance regional collaboration.

This leaves the provinces to look to their present and future interests for incentives for cooperation. If the relatively unadvanced state of regional intergovernmental relations is consequential for western

Canadians—if current or future quality of life issues are significantly affected, if the realization of the region's full promise requires greater coordination—then the argument for action is considerably stronger. It is possible that growing alignment with respect to specific western Canadian policy needs, as identified in chapters 2 and 3, is improving the prospects for a more integrated region. It is also possible that the opportunities and challenges of the global economy, to be discussed further in chapter 5, might increase the incentives for intergovernmental cooperation; it may be that the western provinces could afford not to cooperate in the past but will be unable to afford not to do so in the future. Here we note that while in a Canadian context, relatively small provincial populations and economies are much less of an issue, size may well matter when we shift to a global perspective. For example, Alberta is a reasonably sized Canadian player as the fourth largest province, but it is no more than pocket change in the global economy. More generally, the potential impact of global forces on the case for regional cooperation is still difficult to assess. Asian market demand for western Canadian natural resources could strengthen the push for greater integration, as the government of Alberta would argue, or could weaken it as we have seen in the Northern Gateway and Kinder Morgan disputes.

We realize that we have not made the case for greater regional integration with any great force or consistency and, for that matter, nor have others. There are few notable champions of greater regional integration, and it is not a frequent topic for editorial commentary or talk radio. While we see considerable potential advantages to greater integration, we also recognize that the "durable provincialisms" present in Canada present a formidable barrier. Moreover, the progress that has been made to date has not been driven by a groundswell of public interest or support; the New West Partnership, we suspect, is not well-known within the general public. (Saskatchewan's potential entry into TILMA was hotly debated within the province, but entry into NWPTA stirred up much less controversy.) However, should the western provinces decide to pursue greater integration in the future, they will be able to build on significant if less than overwhelming public attachments to the West as an identity community. It is this topic to which we now turn.

The Attitudinal "Ground": Public Sentiment Underlying the Region

While regions may lack institutional homes, regional identities often develop regardless due to shared histories, economies, and/or geographies. As Anderson notes, "While interregional difference is a social reality, the regional feature of Canada may also exist 'in the minds' of citizens who believe that the collective experience and condition in one geographical area of the country is different than in other parts of the country" (2010, 448). Indeed, in David Smith's evocative prose, Canada's prairies can be seen as "a region of the mind":

> . . . it is at the level of public consciousness that the region
> has achieved its lasting identity. Visually, to anyone traveling
> between the rim of the Shield and the foothills of the Rockies
> across a thousand miles of "black soil sliding into open sky," the
> Prairies merge as one vast land. For those who have never seen
> the Canadian plains but know their history and literature, the
> region is myth, of the mind. . . . (1976, 46)

What is not clear is whether this "region of the mind" extends into British Columbia, whether it continues to exist in the face of the demographic and economic changes noted in chapters 2 and 3, and how it will fare on the turbulent waters of the global economy (to be examined more closely in chapter 5).

The notion of regional identities and regional attitudes has direct public policy relevance. Thus far, we have suggested that the western provinces often quack like regional ducks and occasionally walk like regional ducks (although not for long distances). But, to stretch the analogy further than it should probably be stretched, are the regional ducks walking on solid ground? Stated differently, if the western provinces do wish to pursue regional approaches, are they building on a relatively firm attitudinal foundation that anchors the region within the western Canadian public? Is there a pre-existing attitudinal community, a shared set of perspectives and identities among the residents of the four western provinces that binds them together in some way? If premiers face electorates who do not perceive, relate to, or care about "the West" as a region, any future attempts to institutionalize western Canada as a coherent region, be it through the New West Partnership, the Western Premiers' Conference, or another vehicle, would have only limited support among the electorate. When interprovincial conflict exists, the electorate may even react with hostility to any suggestion that provincial interests are being subjugated to much more abstract regional interests.

While public opinion data in this respect are highly limited, the data that are available suggest that regional identities are present in western Canada: the general public perceives the West to be a distinct region, and identifies with this region. This is not to suggest that regional identities are necessarily strong but rather that there does exist some preliminary basis of attitudinal support—regional attitudinal ground, to continue our metaphor—upon which future regional cooperation efforts might be built. Further, regional identities might find expression in other forms, such as regional discontent, regionally based political parties and regional voting patterns—all matters present throughout western Canadian history (as discussed in chapter 1).

Social group identities can be politically meaningful: politicians can attempt to appeal to political identifications to garner support for their actions, or to invoke opposition to another party or government's actions. Regional identities can be a resource for provincial politicians who wish to incite opposition to a federal policy or who wish to garner support for particular interprovincial cooperation efforts.[8] Regional identities can also be a resource for federal politicians seeking to attack the policy positions of their opponents; a federal party might assert that their opponents have failed to consider regional interests or are even deliberately acting against a particular region. It has often been argued that regional conflict in Canada tends to surpass that of social class, a situation quite different from that south of the border.

However, the mere existence of regional identities should not suggest that they are of sufficient strength to emulate provincial and national identities, and indeed there are many reasons to presume that western Canadian regional identities will be relatively weak. As noted earlier in this chapter, the four provinces lack any true institutional home or even symbols; there are no regional flags, drivers' licences, political parties, or professional sports leagues. (The Western Hockey League is a semi-professional league, and the Canadian Football League's Western Division, much like the New West Partnership, excludes Manitoba's Winnipeg Blue Bombers.) The western provinces each have unique economic and demographic circumstances, which can make it difficult to identify a single *western Canadian* position on any given policy issue. Given this, it is notable, even surprising, that public opinion research shows that many western Canadians see the West in a regional light and that this perception has held over time. In a 1977 public opinion study, roughly four in five respondents across all four provinces felt that there was a "very or moderately strong . . . sense of regional identity" in the West (Goldfarb 1977, 22). The proportion ranged from 77 per cent in Manitoba to 90 per cent in Alberta. Interestingly, this national study found respondents in all provinces reporting strong regional identities, with Atlantic Canada at 78 per cent, Quebec at 86 per cent, and Ontario at 76 per cent.

Regional identities persisted over a quarter of a century later and under very different political and economic circumstances. A 2006 Canada

West Foundation survey, the most recent survey (to our knowledge) to look at regional identities, asked a large sample of western Canadians to rate their closeness to Canada, their province, "the city, town or rural area in which [they] live," and to "western Canada—that is, BC, Alberta, Saskatchewan and Manitoba as a region" (Berdahl 2006, 3). A surprisingly high number of respondents (61.1 per cent) stated that they felt somewhat or very close to western Canada. Indeed, respondents were almost as likely to identify with the region as they were to identify with their local community (64.7 per cent)—a striking finding given the lack of an institutional "home" for western Canada. Regional identifications were strongest in Saskatchewan, where two-thirds of respondents strongly or very strongly identified with the region, and weakest in British Columbia and Manitoba, where nonetheless just under three in five respondents strongly or very strongly identified with the region (Berdahl 2006).[9]

The fact that western Canadians perceive the West as a region is underscored by the Canada West Foundation's 2001 and 2004 surveys, which asked large samples of western Canadians to rate their agreement with the statement, "The West is a distinct region, different in many ways from the rest of Canada" (Berdahl 2004, 9). The surveys found that over 8 in 10 western Canadians strongly or somewhat agreed with the statement, with agreement being slightly higher in Alberta (89 per cent in 2004) and Saskatchewan (90.0 per cent) than in British Columbia (83.1 per cent) and Manitoba (83.5 per cent). Further, the 2004 survey included an Ontario sample where 7 in 10 respondents also strongly or somewhat agreed. While more recent data are not available, it is reasonable to assume that Canadians inside and outside the region continue to perceive "the West" as a distinct region within Canada.

In many ways it is striking that the West—four provinces, each with varying economic fortunes, unique histories, and dynamic political cultures, contained in a vast geography with two very distinct landscapes and climates (prairies and mountains)—manifests itself as a region. Diversity has not prevented a regional identity from taking root. Of course, it is entirely possible that future demographic change—specifically interprovincial migration and immigration to western Canada—may alter feelings of regionalism (Bilodeau, White, and Nevitte 2010) and, by extension, regional identities. Thus, while premiers adopting regional approaches—be it through the Western Premiers' Conference, the New West Partnership, or some other vehicle—may be treading on relatively firm attitudinal ground for now, that ground may shift over time.

Conclusion

Regions tend to take on greater cohesion and homogeneity the farther one moves away. The closer you get to the land and its people, the more the region begins to fragment first into quite distinctive provincial communities and then into a multitude of communities within the provinces themselves. No one, for example, would confuse Estevan with Kamloops or, within British Columbia, Prince George with Victoria. To view a region such as the West up close is like looking into a kaleidoscope where the brightly coloured pieces threaten to overwhelm the regional pattern. Certainly, there are times and circumstances when the focus of discussion is on relatively "mundane" issues of social policy and economic development, and thus regional patterns are difficult to discern; many provincial policy issues are like fine wines that do not travel well. However, there are also times and circumstances when the kaleidoscope is twisted in such a way as to bring regional patterns into bold relief; this happened, we would argue, in the constitutional debates of the 1980s and 1990s. Those circumstances could return if constitutional debate breaks out again, or if the regional dependence on resource extraction runs up against different priorities and values in the rest of Canada.

In this chapter, we have examined the extent to which the four western provincial governments choose to *act* as a region. In doing so, we demonstrated that although the provinces often adopt regional models, these are and will continue to be limited by weak institutionalization. The provinces have room to act in greater unison—doing so is within their jurisdictional capacities and, given the presence of regional identities, there is no reason to presume public opposition to regional approaches. Nevertheless, there is a strong bias for provincial governments to protect provincial autonomies when they do act. As Stephen Tomblin explains,

> [P]rovincialism has survived because provincial actors operate in separate worlds: they play for different audiences, they have access to different resources, and their responses to problems or new policy challenges are guided by inherited policies, assumptions, and past experiences. These policy traditions, deeply embedded in the political culture, and reinforced by province-centered bureaucratic structures and political party systems, have made it difficult for premiers to deal with issues from a regional perspective. (1995, 67)

The "business case" for promoting the regional interest is, to say the least, underdeveloped.

This naturally leads to the question of whether or not the western provinces *should* assume a more formalized institutional model. On the one hand, there is a convincing argument to be made for greater interprovincial cooperation and for the formalization of that cooperation. There are two basic drivers. First, there may be things that the region can do together that individual provinces cannot achieve. One example is the creation of an effective transportation grid that links western Canadian producers to world markets. Lying behind this driver is a basic demographic reality: the western Canadian provinces alone, and for that matter the region as a whole, have a small population base by world or even continental standards. Therefore as the focus of western Canadians shifts from the domestic to the global economy, as discussed in the next chapter, a regional approach may make greater and greater sense.

The second driver for greater cooperation is the realization that what cannot be accomplished through cooperation may have to be accomplished, if it is accomplished at all, through the federal government. As we noted at the start of this chapter, when the three western-most premiers announced the formation of the New West Partnership in 2010, they declared that "with one voice, the West would be a leader on issues that are vital to the nation's competitiveness." Here we would suggest that no issue is more important to the region, and to the country, than energy policy, and in this case *regional* leadership to date has been missing in action. This raises the question of whether the federal government, either current or future, will step in to provide leadership on the issue. In her analysis of federal systems, Bolleyer argues that a lack of coordination by provinces or states promotes the centralization of power. As she writes, "Centralization is accelerated by, if not rooted in, the incapacity of lower level governments to unify, oppose federal plans, and coordinate policy without federal intervention" (2009, 3). She also suggests that the inability of substate governments to coordinate policy without federal intervention presents the federal government with an advantage in the push-pull of federal–provincial relations:

> Lower level governments do not necessarily agree on whether to delegate power (e.g., whether to accept national regulations which are potentially beneficial to lower level governments but touch upon their competencies), a situation which the federal government can easily exploit through pursuing a 'divide-and-rule' strategy. . . . Furthermore, conflicts among or within lower level governments often allow the federal government to act

outside its jurisdiction irrespective of lower level governments' individual or collective preferences, which makes collective monitoring of the federal government all the more important. (2009, 4)

Given the "open federalism" model that now prevails in Ottawa, one that is highly decentralist when it comes to social policy, concerns about federal intrusion are likely not a strong driver at present. However, the open federalism model does not preclude the federal government stepping in and coordinating policy on behalf of provinces; the most immediate test cases are likely to emerge from the swirl of environmental and Aboriginal policies, in part propelled by court decisions mandating a more active federal government role. Here it should also be noted that, at the time of writing, the opposition parties in Parliament favour a much more active federal role in social policy, and even in fields such as education that are deeply embedded in provincial jurisdiction.

While the advantages of policy coordination, combined with the need for provincial action in the absence of an activist federal government, might point toward greater institutionalization of regional bodies, there are also important counterpoints. Specifically, there are very real limits to the potential for interprovincial cooperation. The provinces are competitors for human capital and economic investment, and provincial governments are accountable to provincial taxpayers who often lack a regional policy perspective, or who may oppose regional approaches as a "race to the bottom," a compromising of public policy standards in the interest of cooperation. At issue, then, is whether changes in the economic circumstances of western Canada, and in particular changes in the global economy, will strengthen the business case for regional cooperation and even, to a degree, regional integration. It is to those changing circumstances that we now turn.

Notes

1   We borrow this phrase and idea from Allen (1973).

2   While it is not necessarily an impediment to government action, it must be noted that some scholars argue that interprovincial cooperation undermines governmental transparency and accountability due to the fact that intergovernmental agreements are typically negotiated in camera and documents may be protected from freedom of information laws. See Simeon and Cameron (2002).

3   Of course, not all competition is zero-sum as tourism promotion by individual western provinces might result in increased tourism to other western provinces as tourists combine travel itineraries; the Vancouver–Banff/Calgary corridor is a good example.

4   Executive cooperation includes the Council of the Federation (COF, established in
    2003) and its precursor, the Annual Premiers' Conference (APC). Ministerial meet-
    ings are typically organized around sectoral or line ministries (Simmons 2004);
    more institutionalized examples include the Canadian Councils of Ministers of the
    Environment (CCME) and Forest Ministers (CCFM). Examples of regional minis-
    terial meetings include the Council of Atlantic Ministers of Education and Training
    and the Western Transportation Ministers Council.

5   In 2003, the northern premiers held the first such forum in Nunavut, and signed
    the Northern Cooperation Accord (Yukon, Northwest Territories, and Nunavut
    2007, 2).

6   The AIT, which has established Canada's legal framework for internal trade
    since July 1, 1995, includes Clause 1800 ("Trade Enhancement Arrangements")
    that permits the signatories to "enter into bilateral or multilateral arrangements
    in order to enhance trade and mobility" above the AIT levels (Internal Trade
    Secretariat 2012). It should be noted that provinces were not prohibited from
    entering interprovincial trade agreements prior to the AIT; for example, on April 1,
    1989, the four western provinces signed the "Memorandum of Agreement of the
    Reduction of Internal Trade Barriers in Government Procurement" (available at
    http://www.ait-aci.ca/index_en/progress.htm).

7   TILMA and its successor agreement, the New West Partnership Trade Agreement,
    also helped to advance AIT reform. See Berdahl (2013).

8   We should note that political identities are distinct from political cultures. For
    discussions about regional and provincial political cultures in Canada, we refer
    readers to Schwartz (1974); Simeon and Elkins (1974, 1980); Bell and Tepperman
    (1979); Gibbins (1982); Cooper (2002); Clarke, Pammett, and Stewart (2002);
    Leuprecht (2003); O'Neill and Erickson (2003); Henderson (2004); and Wesley
    (2011).

9   Is there reason for concern that such regional identities might undermine national
    identities? In a word, no. Canadian scholarship has historically treated politi-
    cal identities as being in competition with each other; survey respondents, for
    example, were asked whether they considered themselves to be "Canadians first"
    or "Ontarians first." This approach ran contrary to identity theory and research
    in other countries, which found that individuals are comfortable expressing mul-
    tiple identities at the same time (see, for example, Tajfel et al. 1971; Turner 1978;
    Abrams and Hogg 1999).

5. Western Canada and the World

SOMETIMES, GOVERNMENTS GET it just right. Take, for example, a recent Government of Canada website description of the West:

> Canada's four western provinces are the crossroads between the massive US market and the burgeoning economies of Asia. They are also the nexus for Canada's traditional and new economy.... With the advantages of groundbreaking R&D, regional clusters, highly-skilled people and a strong entrepreneurial spirit, the sky is the limit in big-sky country—Canada's vast prairie and Pacific region. (Canada 2012a)

This crossroads location, however, offers up not only huge opportunities but also quite daunting challenges. If only the world was as simple as Yogi Berra suggested when he said, "When you come to a fork in the road, take it." Western Canadians face a plethora of forks, all shrouded in uncertainty.

To this point we have discussed the West's evolving position within Canada's demography (chapter 2), the national economy (chapter 3), and the political system (chapters 1 and 4). Now we turn to a more elusive topic, and that is the West's place within the global economy—*western Canada and the world*. For some readers this may seem a rather pretentious topic that exaggerates the global importance of the region. After all, only one in every 700 of the world's population lives in western Canada (and only one in every 200 lives in Canada), and thus western Canadians (like Canadians overall) lack the demographic clout to remake the world in their own image. However, the influence of *the world on the West* has been and will continue to be unavoidable and deep. The West's trade in natural resources is increasingly heading toward international markets beyond North America, albeit in the face of strong market-access headwinds, and we would argue that the West's niche within the global economy will be the major factor shaping the region's place within the Canadian economy, and thus within the political system. Therefore any discussion about western Canada and the world will inevitably return to a discussion about the place of the West in Canada.

Furthermore, western Canada's limited capacity to shape the world around it should not lead to the assumption that the external community is indifferent to what is happening in the region and in Canada as a whole. For example, the fact that Canada accounts for only 2 per cent of global greenhouse gas emissions has not let us off the hook with respect to the environmental community. Projects such as the oil sands, pipelines to the United States and across British Columbia, and potential tanker traffic on the west coast are often seen as symbolic battlegrounds even if their objective impact on the global environment is likely to be slight. For those considering travelling to Canada, investing in the Canadian economy, or buying our products, what we do in our own backyard can be highly relevant.

In this chapter we will explore western Canada's position in the global economy, with particular focus on Asia. We will argue that the combination of new Asian markets and investment opportunities, coupled with limited prospects for growth in traditional markets, could transform Canada's regional and national economies. However, new Asian realities will play out quite differently in the western and central Canadian economies, with western Canada being uniquely positioned to benefit from changes in the global economy. At the same time, the ability to access Asian markets and investment will depend very much on supportive public policies, and especially federal policies. Thus, we are brought full circle to the early days of the wheat economy when issues of market access defined the political relationship between the West and the Government of Canada. We will also note that new economic relationships with Asian markets and investors could have far-reaching consequences for the elusive goal of a more diversified regional economy.

Readers should be aware that although we talk in this chapter about "Canada's trade" with the United States or Asia, most of that trade takes place between private firms, including state-owned enterprises, rather than between countries. National governments play a significant role in creating the channels along which trade flows and the barriers that inhibit such trade, but they are not active traders themselves. Canada, in the sense of the Government of Canada, sells very little, with the exception of the Canadian Wheat Board (past more than present) and the ongoing engagement of Atomic Energy of Canada Ltd., both arms-length Crown corporations. Provincial governments in the West have recently become active players in promoting global market access, but they too, with the notable exception of provincial crown corporations (e.g., BC Hydro, Manitoba Hydro, Quebec Hydro), are neither sellers nor buyers in the international marketplace. The use of country names (or provincial names, for that matter) is a convenient shorthand for what are extraordinarily complex trading relationships; it has been less "the West" that has been searching for greater market access than it has been thousands of individual producers located within the region.

Western Canada: A Trading Region within a Trading Nation

Right from the get-go, Canada has been a trading nation, blessed with an abundance of resources but limited by a relatively small domestic market. From beaver skins, tall timbers, and wheat, from nickel, pulp, and cod, and more recently from minivans to BlackBerries, potash, oil, and uranium, Canadians produced far more than could be absorbed by the domestic market. Unlike the United States with its huge internal market, easily 10 times the size of Canada's, our prosperity has been dependent on the ability to sell in the international marketplace, and to sell not only resources but the entire gamut of goods and services associated with a modern, knowledge-based economy. Nowhere has this challenge been more acute than in the West.

For Canadians, *international* trade has been primarily *American* trade: exports to the United States, imports from the United States, and American investments in the Canadian economy. The key international relationship for Canada as a whole, and for the West, is with the United States. The majority of western Canadian exports are destined for the US, although dependency on US markets varies considerably, from a high of 83 per cent of Alberta exports being US-bound to a low of 50 per cent for British Columbia (Roach 2010, 116; 2009 data). This regional reliance on American markets, which is not out of line with the national pattern, has been largely positive. Proximity to the world's largest economy, a highly permeable if not entirely undefended border, the absence of other neighbours, a common business culture and language (at least for most Canadians), and similar legal systems all encourage a close economic relationship. There is nothing new about this observation. However, neither the relationship with the United States nor the broader patterns of international trade and investment within which that relationship is embedded play out uniformly across the country. Canada has a loosely integrated set of *regional* economies more than it has a strong *national* economy, a reality that can be illustrated by a rough and ready review of the economic histories of Ontario and the West.

The Ontario Experience

As we discussed in chapter 1, and to paint here with a *very* broad brush, the tariffs put into place by the 1879 National Policy were designed to protect an infant manufacturing sector from foreign and particularly American competition; similar tariff strategies were ubiquitous across the western world until well after the end of World War II. In Canada's case, tariff protection was not only reasonably effective, it also encouraged American firms to "jump the tariff wall" by setting up branch plants north of the border, plants that were then protected by Canadian tariffs: for example, DuPont Canada, Ford Canada, GE Canada, GM Canada, and scores more. The result was a robust manufacturing sector in Ontario (and Quebec) that was highly integrated with the manufacturing sector in the United States, particularly with those firms located in adjoining states.[1] The best illustration of this very close relationship was the 1965 Auto Pact that all but erased the Canada–US border as far as (and only as far as) the automotive industry was concerned. The national origin of parts and autos, and the national location of plants and assembly lines, were of little consequence, and thus Ontario was able to develop a larger and more muscular auto industry than the domestic Canadian market alone could have supported.

For most of the last century, therefore, and with the exception of the Auto Pact, promoting greater free trade through lower tariffs had little allure for Ontario manufacturers, including the array of branch plants that had grown up behind the tariff wall. The sector's priority was to protect the domestic Canadian market, including emerging markets in western Canada; the big prize was access to and integration with the American economy. The Canadian automotive industry, for example, did not sell and did not need to sell outside the continental market; if Ford or GM vehicles were sold in Europe or Japan, they were manufactured abroad or sold through the US parent.

It was only when access to the American market was jeopardized by growing congressional protectionism in the early 1980s that support grew in Ontario for what became the 1989 Free Trade Agreement (FTA) with the United States, and the 1993 North American Free Trade Agreement (NAFTA) with the United States and Mexico. Beyond securing continental market access it was hoped that tariff reductions would make Canadian manufacturers more productive, thus opening up the possibility of greater international sales beyond North America. It was also hoped, and slowly realized, that non-tariff *interprovincial* barriers to trade and labour mobility would come down along with tariffs, thereby expanding the internal market.

We have to be careful, of course, not to reduce Ontario's economy to manufacturing alone. Mineral extraction, particularly in the "ring of fire" area in northwestern Ontario, remains a strong part of the province's complex economic mix, and mineral extraction has fostered engineering, financial, and legal expertise that is marketed around the world, making Toronto a global player in the mining sector. Ontario, and more specially Toronto, dominates Canada's financial industry. Agriculture, focused primarily on the province's large urban markets, has by no means disappeared. Nor should it be assumed that the Ontario economy is locked into continental markets alone. Ontario financial institutions, pharmaceutical companies, and high-tech innovators have often been very successful in broader international markets; think, for example, of the global impact of Research in Motion (now known as BlackBerry Limited) and its BlackBerry smartphone in the first decade of the twenty-first century.

Nonetheless, manufacturing is the flagship of the Ontario economy, and in recent years the manufacturing sector in Ontario, like its counterparts in Europe and the United States, has faced growing competition from booming and relatively low-wage Asian economies. Sustaining a prosperous manufacturing sector has become increasingly difficult, particularly in the Canadian case where, unlike the US and EU, there is not a large domestic market. Thus, the dramatic growth of the Asian economies has been viewed in Ontario, albeit not universally, as a threat to the manufacturing sector rather than as an expanded market for goods and services. This shift in the global economy and its domestic implications play out quite differently in the West.

The Western Canadian Experience

Again to paint with a very broad brush, whereas Ontario producers were reluctant and late free trade supporters, western Canadian producers, especially on the prairies, were always much more enthusiastic about knocking down tariff walls and promoting greater free trade. After all, the tariffs that protected manufacturers in Ontario meant higher input costs and very few benefits for the agrarian community. Farmers could not purchase lower cost equipment from the United States but were instead channelled by tariff policy to purchase higher cost equipment from Canadian manufacturers, thus putting them at a disadvantage when they competed with American farmers on world markets. Because tariffs can only be imposed on imports, an export-driven resource economy cannot be protected by tariff walls.

Unlike their manufacturing counterparts in Ontario, western Canadian exporters, particularly in the early years of the wheat economy, had no choice but to look beyond continental markets. Although such markets were (and are) important to the West—99 per cent of oil, gas, and petroleum exports go to the US, as does most dimensional lumber—the prosperity of the region also depended on international markets for such products as metallurgical coal, potash, pulse crops, uranium, and wheat. In many of these cases, Americans were and remain competitors more than markets. Western Canadians therefore tended to be free traders through and through, and it is not surprising that Alberta Premier Peter Lougheed was a leading proponent for the FTA and NAFTA.

But, that was then and this is now. Economic circumstances in western Canada have changed quite dramatically:

- In large part due to the Organization of Petroleum Exporting Countries (OPEC), from the mid-1970s onward energy resources commanded much higher albeit volatile prices in domestic, continental, and global markets.
- More generally, the *terms of trade* for western commodities—that is, the relative purchasing power of a unit of resource production[2]—increased across the board after decades of decline.
- The omnipresent wheat economy in the prairie West slowly gave way to a much more diversified range of crops within which wheat was but one of many commodities sold on the international market.
- Although agricultural output in the West grew steadily in the decades following World War II, the size of the agricultural labour force shrank and western Canada became heavily urbanized.
- Potash and heavy oil joined the basket of export commodities.

In many ways, the regional economy became more diversified across a range of natural resource industries, a transformation that opened up even broader engagement with the global economy. Although this economic transformation did not bring the regional economy into alignment with the Ontario economy, the earlier conflicts over tariff policies disappeared in a new free trade environment shaped by GATT (the General Agreement on Tariffs and Trade), the FTA, and NAFTA.

Ontario and the West: Shared Vulnerability

The structural differences between the regional economies in Ontario and western Canada should not conceal a shared dependency on the United States. American markets and investment have driven resource development as much as they have driven other sectors of the Canadian economy, including manufacturing. Both regions are therefore vulnerable to episodic and perhaps growing protectionist sentiment in the United States. Both require costly physical infrastructure—highways, border crossings, pipelines, and bridges (the proposed second Windsor–Detroit bridge carries a price tag of $5.5 billion)—to link Canadian producers to markets south of the border. American security concerns that threaten to "thicken" the border pose a risk to both regional economies, although perhaps less so for the West's bulk exports of natural resources than for Ontario's trade in manufactured parts and products. Indeed, those very concerns have been used to promote Canada as a safe and secure source of energy supplies for the United States. Nevertheless, if the American economy weakens, the demand for Canadian imports tends to weaken across the economy: hence the mantra that "when the American economy catches a cold, the Canadian economy catches pneumonia," although during the 2008–11 recession, Canada escaped with only a light chill.

This vulnerability to the health of the American economy, and to swings in American trade policy, can be illustrated by country-of-origin legislation for retail foods, the 2002 increase in American agricultural subsidies, American fuel standards, opposition in states such as California to the consumption of Canadian (but not American) heavy oil, and the softwood lumber dispute, a Canada–US trade dispute that primarily affected British Columbia, which supplies 50 per cent of Canada's softwood lumber exports. (The softwood lumber dispute was addressed through the 2006 Softwood Lumber Agreement, which was renewed in 2012.) A more recent example is the increasingly precarious state of oil and gas exports to the United States. Faltering demand in the face of episodic downturns in the American business cycle has always been a fact of life, but in the future American demand may be flat even in the best of times as consumption falls in the face of new fuel standards, technological change, and environmental policy. At the same time as American demand weakens, American production of shale gas and tight oil has soared, thus reducing dependency on and perhaps even interest in Canadian imports. Energy independence for the United States is no longer a pipe dream.

On top of this gloomy supply and demand situation, environmentalists in the United States have vigorously opposed increased Canadian pipeline access to American markets, the most prominent example being

the pitched battle against TransCanada's proposed Keystone XL pipeline that would deliver bitumen from Alberta to refineries on the Gulf
Coast of Texas. This combination of falling American demand, increasing American supply, and market access challenges is deeply troubling
for the Canadian oil and gas industry, and for the regional economy writ
large. Although Ontario exports to the United States are not immune to
swings in the American business cycle, they are less exposed on other
fronts than are exports from western Canada. To date, manufactured
exports have not been targeted by environmental organizations in the
United States; a much greater threat for Ontario's manufacturing sector
has come from American state subsidies designed to attract new manufacturing opportunities.

Since September 11, 2001, although perhaps coincidentally, we have
seen growing protectionism in the United States, a movement that potentially affects a broad swath of western Canadian exports running from
softwood lumber to beef, pork, and a range of agricultural products.
Here the West's reliance on American markets carries with it a growing vulnerability to protectionist measures that it was hoped NAFTA
would deter. To date, however, the protection provided by NAFTA has
been modest. Certainly NAFTA offers little if any protection from environmental activism or from the indirect impact of domestic American
environmental initiatives on Canadian–American trade.

In short, the American market is not secure and can no longer be
taken for granted. Of course, it will always be important to Canada,
and to the West; the American economy is simply too big and too close
for it to be anything else. However, Canadian opportunities for *growth*
will be found elsewhere, and particularly in Asia. The US and the EU
are unlikely to be high-growth regions, and in both cases Canada's challenge will be to maintain rather than increase market share in the face of
an increasingly competitive global economy. Africa and South America
offer strong prospects for domestic economic growth, but are more
likely to provide competition for Canadian resource sales than markets
for Canadian goods, especially resources coming from the West.

The West Looks to Asia

In the face of American market vulnerability, and in the pursuit of
economic growth, western Canadians may have little option but to
double-down on Asia. The smaller manufacturing base in the West is not
threatened by Asian competition, and Asia offers the prospect of new,
potentially vast markets for natural resources along with the investment needed by an expanding resource sector. It is also anticipated that

western Canadians will be able to secure a higher price for commodity exports on international markets than on continental markets. In the words of Alberta Premier Alison Redford, "It's fundamental to us to be able to get our product to tidewater, to open up international markets and make sure we get a much better price for our resource" (Wood 2013). Seldom does reliance on a single buyer yield optimal results for sellers, and world prices for oil and natural gas routinely exceed continental prices. Thus, Asian economic growth is generally welcomed in the West while it encounters a more guarded reception in Ontario. After all, manufacturing and financial services jobs can be outsourced to Asia in a way that resource extraction cannot.

In chapter 3 we discussed the westward drift of the Canadian economy, the slow but steady movement of employment, investment, head offices, and wealth to the four western provinces. The centre of the global economy is also drifting in the same direction, toward Asia and at a clip considerably greater than the more sedate Canadian transformation. What we don't know yet is whether the global transformation will reinforce or accelerate economic change in Canada, and change in the regional balance of the national economy. Are western Canadians better positioned than other Canadians to cash in on global economic change? Will the West be more attractive than other regions for Asian investment?

Western Canadians are quick to believe—perhaps too quick—that because they have the energy, food, and minerals that the world wants and needs, the world will beat a path to their door. As the global population grows from seven to nine billion over the next two decades, and as consumer demand expands in increasingly affluent developing countries such as China and India, the global demand for what we produce should only grow. However, without *access* to new markets the resources that the West holds in such abundance could be stranded, just so much stuff in and on the ground, or at best subject to the whims of American markets increasingly awash in much that the West produces.

Fortunately, western Canada and particularly British Columbia have a number of cards to play when it comes to building an expanded relationship with Asian economies that reach well beyond China to include Japan (currently Canada's largest Asian trading partner), South Korea, Taiwan, and Vietnam. (Sometimes but not always, India gets casually tossed into the "Asian" mix.) One is simple proximity; in the words of recent advertising by the Government of British Columbia, "Canada begins here." Vancouver is two days closer by sea to Shanghai than is Los Angeles, and Prince Rupert is three days closer. British Columbia also has large immigrant communities from across Asia, communities that could form the interpersonal bridges across which a good deal of trade tends to flow. Post-secondary institutions in British Columbia, and increasingly in Alberta, have been developing strong Asian ties.

Furthermore, there is nothing new in the West about an economic relationship with Asia. Chinese workers were instrumental in the construction of the Canadian Pacific Railway in the 1880s, John Diefenbaker's Progressive Conservative government opened up Chinese markets for Canadian wheat in the late 1950s, and Japan has been a strong market for Canadian metallurgical coal and timber for decades. The western provinces, and particularly British Columbia, already have relatively strong export relationships with China and Japan; almost 11 per cent of western Canadian merchandise exports in 2009 were destined for those two countries, compared to 2.5 per cent of exports from the rest of Canada. While the western figure is strongly inflated by British Columbia, with almost 24 per cent of its exports directed to Japan and China, the three prairie provinces all exceeded the non-western Canada rate by a considerable margin (Alberta 6 per cent, Saskatchewan almost 10 per cent, Manitoba 11 per cent) (Roach 2010, 115).

At the same time, western Canada faces a number of significant challenges in expanding Asian markets and attracting Asian investment. The convergence of Canadian and Asian economic growth is not preordained, and there is nothing inevitable about either continued Asian economic growth (Chang 2011) or the West's ability to ride the Asian economic wave. Rather than waiting for Asian markets and investors to beat a path to our door, we will have to do much of the beating.

Hard Infrastructure

The hard infrastructure needed for western Canadian producers to reach international markets of any stripe, and indeed for Canadian producers generally to reach those markets, faces daunting environmental, financial, and logistical challenges. Although the infrastructure for the bulk of north-south trade with the United States is largely in place, improvements are always needed, and thus we see significant federal government investment in border crossings and meeting American security needs. However, increasing pipeline capacity will be a challenge, as the controversy over the Keystone XL expansion so graphically illustrates, and new high voltage transmission lines potentially face similar opposition. Nonetheless, and even keeping the Keystone XL experience in mind, the hard infrastructure challenges with respect to north-south trade pale when compared to those confronting expanded trade with Asia.

Most Canadian products bound for Asian markets, and Asian products bound for North American markets, require port facilities on the west coast along with the roads, railways, and pipelines stretching back from the ports to the point of production or, in the case of Asian imports, to the point of consumption. The intense controversy that emerged in 2012 over the proposed Northern Gateway pipeline to carry bitumen from Alberta to tankers on the west coast, and the similar if somewhat more muted controversy over the proposed expansion of Kinder Morgan Canada's existing TransMountain pipeline running from Edmonton to port facilities near Vancouver, illustrate just how difficult market access can be. Proposed projects may encounter significant although by no means universal First Nation opposition (Vanderklippe 2013), and at the very least demands for revenue sharing from First Nations, municipal authorities, and perhaps even provincial governments. As we discussed in chapter 3, environmental opposition may stem not only from site-specific concerns about air pollution (particularly coal dust in the Lower Mainland of British Columbia), ground water contamination, river crossings, and tanker safety, but also from the conviction that Asian consumption of western Canadian resources, such as coal from British Columbia, will increase global warming. The export challenge, then, is both logistical and moral.

Now, the hard infrastructure challenges facing bitumen exports are undoubtedly greater than the challenges facing other exports, in part but only in part because the former are so thoroughly entangled in debates about global warming and the future of a hydrocarbon-based economy. Nevertheless, the challenges facing bitumen exports are by no means unique. Although opposition to natural gas pipelines is not as intense, particularly among Coastal First Nations, the logistical challenges of extracting the gas in an environmentally acceptable fashion, moving it to the coast, building liquefied natural gas (LNG) port capacity, and shipping LNG to Asia are immense. Moving timber, coal, and other minerals is far from trouble-free—coal exports through the Port of Vancouver are becoming particularly contentious—and agricultural trade increasingly needs just-in-time delivery so that niche producers can connect with demanding Asian buyers. In many cases it is difficult to see how these infrastructure challenges can be met without significant public sector engagement, perhaps not as a funder but certainly as an active player in the negotiations with communities and First Nations.

Soft Infrastructure

Not all trade needs hard infrastructure. For example, the engineering, environmental, financial, and legal expertise that hundreds of BC firms provide to the global mining industry does not require ports and tankers, nor does the trade in software and graphic design. Investment flows into the Canadian economy do not require planes, trains, or automobiles, although convenient air travel is an advantage. Nevertheless, virtually all trade requires "soft infrastructure" that is, at best, a work in progress in western Canada.

Trade and investment relationships require more than "stuff" to exchange. They are often built upon personal relationships, and require language skills and at least a basic cultural understanding of one's partners. They benefit from knowledge of national differences in legal systems and business practices. In all of these respects, Canadians have been spoiled by the trade relationship with the United States where the soft infrastructure to make the relationship work is in place as part of a shared culture. When it comes to Asia, the soft infrastructure is still rudimentary, and the existing capacity for language and cross-cultural training may not be sufficient to support any substantial expansion of Asian trade and investment. Canadian governments have concentrated on providing immigrants with the skills they need to prosper in Canada but have spent much less time and energy providing Canadian students, workers, and the business community with the skills they will need to connect with Asia. Here there is certainly a role for universities and colleges, a role that is being met unevenly across the region, and across Canada.

Competition

Western Canada may have what the world wants and needs, but the region is by no means the only potential supplier. Asian demand for natural gas, for example, could be met in large part through LNG exports from Australia and Qatar, through new pipelines from Russia and the former Soviet republics, or through LNG exports from Alaska, all of which offer even greater proximity than does western Canada. The point here is simple but essential: Canada is not alone when it comes to abundant natural resources, and if we are slow to develop the necessary export (and import) infrastructure, both hard and soft, we may be too late. To adapt the tagline from *Field of Dreams,* if we build it, we cannot be sure they will come, but if we don't build it, they certainly won't. Our niche in the global economy is not a birthright; it must be earned, and earned again.

Trade Agreements

International trade is increasingly shaped by multilateral and bilateral trade agreements such as the General Agreement on Tariffs and Trade (GATT), NAFTA, the emergent Trans-Pacific Partnership (TPP), and the Canada–EU Comprehensive Economic and Trade Agreement (CETA), among many, many others. As a consequence, Canada's Asian trade potential will depend in part and perhaps in large part on how Canada is positioned within these international agreements, and indeed whether Canada is even a member of regional trade agreements. Success or failure on this front lies in the hands of the Government of Canada. Although provincial governments are necessarily at the table to some degree in the negotiation of international trade agreements, given that such agreements inevitably touch on areas of provincial responsibility, the federal government is both the initiator and the driving force.

Trade Promotion

Western Canada is a small player on the international stage with, as noted above, only one person in 700 of the global population living in the region. As a consequence, we should expect that international knowledge of the region's strengths, bounty, and beauty will be slight. Increased knowledge will only come through promotional efforts by Canadians; the world will not come looking.

On April 30, 2010, as part of the broader New West Partnership discussed in chapter 4, British Columbia, Alberta, and Saskatchewan signed the New West Partnership International Cooperation Agreement, a non-binding commitment to work together on international trade promotion and marketing. The provinces followed up on this agreement with concrete action: within weeks of signing the agreement, the premiers of the three provinces went on a joint trade mission to China and Japan, and opened a joint trade and investment office in Shanghai. They followed this with a joint trade mission to China and Japan in October 2010 to promote western Canadian agriculture and aquaculture, and in September 2012, despite changes in premiers and some important differences of opinion between the British Columbia and Alberta premiers regarding the proposed Northern Gateway pipeline, the three western premiers co-hosted a reception in China at the World Economic Forum.

Although provincial engagement in international marketing is not new, these efforts suggest a larger effort by the three western provinces to promote western Canada *as a region* on the global stage. Rather than presenting themselves internationally as three separate economies, the three provinces are promoting a single economic unit, "a seamless economic region of nine million people with a combined GDP of more than $550 billion" and "substantial natural resources such as gold, copper, potash, wood, natural gas and metallurgical coal as well as Western Canada's geographical advantage as North America's Pacific Gateway with direct access by rail, air and highway to major North American markets" (Alberta, British Columbia, and Saskatchewan 2010b). In the words of Saskatchewan Premier Brad Wall, "The West has the resources the world needs, we have the opportunities global investors want, and the New West Partnership is making it as easy as possible to access them" (Alberta, British Columbia, and Saskatchewan 2010b).

International trade promotion, including trade missions and the establishment of trade and investment offices in foreign markets, serves both economic and political purposes. Although there is limited empirical evidence supporting the effectiveness of export promotion programs, trade promotion is argued to help reduce information costs for firms considering new markets (Copeland 2008; Head and Ries 2010; Van Biesebroeck, Yu, and Chen 2010). International trade promotion also has political benefits: by engaging in trade missions, governments can build and reinforce relationships with international governments and actors, and can be seen by their electorates as taking steps to promote and build their economies. Further, political leaders can use trade missions to bolster their appearance as "statesmen."

For all of these reasons, trade promotion is an essential part of any western Canadian–Asian strategy. It can come through business associations such as the Business Council of Manitoba, the Business Council of British Columbia, and the Canadian Association of Petroleum Producers; through municipal and First Nation trade missions; and through academic exchanges including student exchanges. Above all else, however, is trade and investment promotion by the Government of Canada. The Canadian "brand" is a major asset for western Canadian firms and governments seeking to expand Asian trade and investment opportunities. It is essential, therefore, but far from assured, that the West has a prominent place in the images of Canada presented by the Government of Canada to the world community. When the world clicks "Canada," more than Toronto and Montreal should pop up on the screen.

A potential constraint on the effectiveness of trade promotion, and one of particular relevance to the West, comes from Canada's international environmental reputation. If, and we stress *if,* we are in a situation where the Canadian stories the world hears are largely about environmental conflict—about the oil sands, tanker traffic off the west coast, Aboriginal land claim disputes, and threats to the well-being of caribou or polar bears—then it will be difficult to get effective traction through trade promotion. What we do domestically on the environmental front, or with respect to international agreements, may damage the Canadian brand, assuming that environmental values trump or at least compete with resource needs in the markets we are targeting. This challenge of environmental and reputational management falls with greatest impact on western Canada where the internationalization of environmental issues—the oil sands, coal exports, the Keystone XL and Northern

Gateway pipeline proposals—has been more pronounced than in other regions.

Plan B: Looking beyond Asia

What happens to the western Canadian economy if the Asian potential does not materialize? What happens if the Asian economies are unable to sustain high levels of economic growth, if Asian demand for agricultural products, coal, lumber, potash, and uranium falls, if pipelines cannot be built to the west coast, if we are beaten to the trading punch by our competitors?

Here the energy sector provides a window on short-term solutions. If Asian markets cannot be opened up for oil and gas, and if American demand weakens in the face of burgeoning domestic supply and falling domestic consumption, then western Canadian producers will of necessity try to expand Canadian markets. Here the main prize would be to replace imported oil and gas in Quebec with oil from western Canada. (As noted in chapter 3, the oil for Quebec and Atlantic markets has primarily come from non-Canadian sources, including the North Sea, Venezuela, and the Middle East.) Greater west–east pipeline capacity would also open up the possibility of western Canadian oil moving offshore through Atlantic ports to Indian markets, and through the Panama Canal to Asian markets. However, while this substitution would make sense on many fronts, including security of supply for Canadians, it cannot be assured. Additional pipeline capacity would still have to be built or existing pipelines re-purposed, and there is no guarantee that either would get through the regulatory process. The Quebec government may not be enthusiastic either because of the perception of "dirty oil" coming in from the oil sands, or because of an interest in protecting the Quebec market for potential oil and gas production in the St. Lawrence Valley. For natural gas, cheaper supplies may be available from American producers. In any event, the Quebec market would be too small to soak up surplus western Canadian production, and could well be a declining market at that. The conclusion is clear: expanding the domestic market for western Canadian oil and gas would help, but not much.

If we turn from oil and gas to other products from the regional economy, the prospects for expanded domestic consumption are even bleaker. While Canada's imports of oil and gas from foreign suppliers could at least hypothetically be displaced by Canadian production, this is not the case for coal, grain, lumber, potash, and uranium, to name but a few. The prospects for growth, especially in the long term, are all to be found offshore. If Plan A is greater access to growing Asian markets and investment capacity, it is not at all clear what Plan B might be other than sharp reductions in regional growth and national prosperity.

Summary

Asian markets and investment will be critically important determinants of *long-term* growth and prosperity in western Canada. This is not to deny the still large, still dominant trading relationship with the United States, one that will overshadow all others in the foreseeable future. However, over-dependence on US trade and investment leaves Canada vulnerable to swings in the American business cycle and public policy, and to swings in American domestic supply of Canadian export commodities. It is also becoming increasingly apparent that the opportunities for growth in American markets are limited, that the best opportunities for growth, particularly with respect to natural resource markets, are to be found in Asia. Unfortunately, there is nothing assured about success in accessing Asian markets and investment.

Building a Supportive Public Policy Framework

Virtually all trade and investment in most western states is private in character; governments today, apart from sovereign wealth funds, are seldom directly involved in selling, buying, or investing. In addition, western Canadian producers of coal, dimensional lumber, natural gas, oil, potash, and uranium are essentially price takers rather than price setters in international trade, making it very difficult to get off the roller coaster of international commodity prices. Both these observations suggest serious limitations on the capacity of public policy to shape Canada's position in the global economy. Nevertheless, public policy frameworks, both federal and provincial, do matter if only at the margins of a global trading system. Certainly success in cracking Asian markets could depend very much on a supportive policy framework that embraces but reaches beyond infrastructure challenges, and on an ideological willingness to employ public policy in the pursuit of economic goals, for this may well be a situation where a market economy alone will not take us where we want to go.

In the past, the principal pathways to foreign markets for western Canadian producers led through Ottawa. Parliament set freight rates for the intercontinental railways linking western Canadian producers to those markets. Regulatory approval for pipelines lay with the National Energy Board. The Government of Canada led trade promotion efforts, and the Canadian Wheat Board was the monopoly international marketer for wheat and barley produced in the western provinces (but not wheat and barley produced in Ontario). It was also the Wheat Board that opened up agricultural markets in China and Russia at the height of the Cold War. The federal government, in collaboration with the United States, built the St. Lawrence Seaway in the 1950s, thereby strengthening Canadian trade routes to Europe and the east coast of the United States. Today, the federal government negotiates international trade agreements such as NAFTA, manages international relationships, and typically takes the lead in international trade promotion; here a striking example is provided by the 2011 Canada–US Beyond the Border Agreement on Travel, Trade and Security. While provinces do play a role in all of these dimensions, the importance of the federal government to western Canada's trade future is difficult to overstate. As a consequence, when western Canadians look for policy tools to improve market access, they look first and foremost to Ottawa, and thus a regional preoccupation with access to foreign markets prompts a focus on the federal government.

In recent decades it may appear that the role of the federal government has diminished somewhat as Canadians have placed greater reliance on markets, and as ideological constraints on government action have grown. Nonetheless, the ongoing importance of the Government of Canada and federal policy can be illustrated across a number of fronts:

- The Government of Canada sets the rules governing foreign investment across the economy, including the potential role of state-owned enterprises (SOEs) in the resource sector. This became a highly contentious issue in 2012 when the federal cabinet approved the $6 billion purchase of Progress Energy Resources by Malaysia's national energy company, Petronas, and the $15.1 billion purchase of Nexen by the China National Offshore Oil Corporation (CNOOC). A December 2012 IPSOS Reid online survey of 1,021 national respondents found that 68 per cent believed that "the Conservative government should block the sale of Canadian firms to *all foreign investors*," and 74 per cent believed the federal government "should stop such proposed acquisitions if they are made by state-owned enterprises" (Kennedy 2012). At the same time, 61 per cent of the survey respondents supported increasing trade with Asia, a percentage that dropped to 51 per cent when *China* was substituted for *Asia*.
- As the importance of north-south trade has increased substantially for all four western provinces, the management of the Canadian–American relationship has also become more important. Management issues extend from the mechanics of border transactions and specific issues such as softwood lumber, fisheries, agricultural subsidies, environmental protection, and pipelines to mega-policy issues such as continental

defence and homeland security. This management still lies, and quite likely inevitably lies, primarily in the hands of the federal government even though the costs imposed by disputes may not be borne equally by all regions of Canada.

- To facilitate trade, governments have an important role to play with respect to transportation, although for the most part that role is regulatory rather than financial. The federal government does not build, own, or operate pipelines; is no more than a rent-collector in terms of airports; no longer owns railways or sets freight rates; and provides only some highway funding (primarily through economic stimulus packages). The direct financial role of the federal government is more pronounced with respect to north-south border infrastructure, and with respect to port infrastructure through such initiatives as the Asia-Pacific Gateway Initiative. More generally, the federal government, through its responsibilities relating to international trade, interprovincial trade, and environmental protection, remains a major player within the transportation systems that link western Canadian producers to domestic and international markets.

- The regulatory impact of the federal government is brought into sharp relief by pipeline projects. Pipeline permitting, for example, flows through the National Energy Board (NEB), and federal environmental assessment regulations, including those relating to inland waters, endangered species, and migratory birds, are brought into play. In 2012 and 2013, the NEB conducted regulatory hearings into the proposed Northern Gateway pipeline that would carry bitumen from Alberta to Kitimat, en route to Asian markets. The NEB does not have the final say in such projects; its recommendations are made to the federal cabinet. The NEB's role in the Northern Gateway project is only the small although by no means insignificant tip of much greater federal policy engagement with resource developments in western Canada.

- In 2012 and 2013 the prime minister was increasingly active in the Asia Pacific region, with a particular focus on Canada's economic relationship with India and China, and on Canada's potential participation in the Trans-Pacific Partnership.

Overall, when it comes to international trade and investment, the federal government is an active player, and may become an even more active player as federal disengagement from social policy is offset by greater interest in economic management. The bottom line for western Canadians is that what happens in Ottawa still counts, and therefore the need for an effective regional voice in Ottawa remains.

At this point some readers may be confused by our focus on federal policy and apparent neglect of provincial policy frameworks.

The latter are undoubtedly central to the terms, conditions, and pace of resource development, but are less so to the challenges of market access. Furthermore, although the federal government relinquished ownership of natural resources to the three prairie provinces in 1930, and although provincial ownership was underscored in the 1982 *Constitution Act,* ownership of natural resources cannot be equated with control over their development. The federal government retains a multitude of powers that can be legitimately brought to bear on resource development. These include not only broad taxation powers, but also jurisdictional authority with respect to interprovincial and international trade, and regulatory authority with respect to environmental protection and foreign investment.

Control of natural resources is inherently more muddied than is ownership. Moreover, resource ownership is of limited value if market access cannot be found, and provincial ownership will neither open Asian markets nor ensure access to traditional markets in the United States. It will not shore up slumping American demand for hydrocarbons, or forestall the almost explosive growth in the American production of natural gas and oil. Constitutional ownership will not ensure the massive amount of foreign investment that will be required, or determine who might be able to invest in Canadian resource development. Provincial resource ownership is a fundamental constitutional principle, but it is only the starting point in resource development and market access.

Federal regulatory powers with respect to environmental protection, along with the federal government's international treaty power, mean that the federal government will largely determine Canada's international environmental brand. If this brand is negative within significant parts of the international community, or is negative for consumers in major markets for Canadian products, then resource investment and development in western Canada will be adversely affected. Canada's positioning on such issues as global warming is part and parcel of Canada's positioning within the international economy. This is not to say that the environmental policies and actions of provincial governments are irrelevant, but only to stress that Canada's brand rests primarily in the hands of the federal government.

Closely related to this is Ottawa's inescapable entanglement with First Nations, and with Aboriginal land claims and treaty rights. Aboriginal peoples, including the Inuit, Metis and non-status Indians, argue that their resource ownership was never relinquished by the treaties, and that provincial ownership of natural resources is contingent on the negotiation of Aboriginal claims. Regardless of how this extraordinarily complex issue is resolved by the courts, Aboriginal communities will face the same reality that provincial governments confront today: resource ownership does not equal resource control, and thus there is no guarantee that resource ownership alone will unlock economic prosperity for Aboriginal communities. Markets must still be found, and the encompassing federal and provincial governments will continue to exercise significant influence on Aboriginal resource development regardless of court expansions of Aboriginal resource ownership. If the Alberta government and the huge oil and gas industry are encountering significant market access challenges, these will be even more difficult for small First Nations in remote parts of the country.

Finally, and as noted in chapter 3, the federal government has had an ongoing if modest interest in economic diversification in western Canada, an interest shared with provincial governments. In many ways, potential Asian markets address the holy grail of greater economic diversification, in this case diversification of markets more than diversification of export products. However, as the Crusaders found out a thousand years ago, holy grails can be maddeningly elusive. A major challenge in the decades to come is whether a deeper relationship with the Asian economies will help or hinder diversification. In terms of markets, there is no question that greater diversification will result if dependency on American markets is reduced. (The same conclusion undoubtedly applies to diversification with respect to foreign investment, although here the impact of federal policies remains to be seen.) What is far less certain is the potential impact of greater Asian trade on western Canadian efforts to move up the value chain, to move from exporting resources in a raw, unprocessed fashion to their more processed form—from logs to dimensional lumber and building materials, bitumen to petroleum, grain to processed food. The goal is to create more high-end jobs in Canada, to move from being hewers of wood and drawers of water to being producers of end products for the global marketplace.

The problem here is that western Canada's relatively weak position in that marketplace limits the ability of western producers to impose their will, to say they will only sell at the top end of the value chain. As noted earlier, western Canadian producers are price-takers rather than price-setters when it comes to international trade; alone or in concert, they do not have the market power to set the price for oil or natural gas, or even for uranium or potash where the region's market share is much larger. And, the West may have more competition at the top end of the value chain than at the bottom end. The unfortunate reality is that Canada's customers are also interested in creating and retaining high-end jobs and would be quite happy to import Canadian resources in a relatively raw form. Expanded Asian trade may therefore prolong and deepen the region's dependence on resource extraction, thus returning us to a very big and difficult question: what does the West do when the resources run out, or when changes in technology and social values erode consumer demand for many of the resources the region has in such abundance?

Conclusion

Western Canada's connections to the global economy, and to the associated larger patterns of cultural and political change, will always be a work in progress. It will also be a critically important work. Throughout this chapter we have argued that the West's global positioning will largely determine the West's place within Canada, that western Canada's success in the global economy will determine in large part the region's place within the Canadian economy and political system. This relationship, moreover, is likely to be reciprocal as the West's place within the national policy architecture will help determine the region's success or failure in building new relationships in the global economy, particularly expanded relationships with Asia. This points to the continued need for an effective regional voice in Ottawa. Even though other ways—including the Internet—are now allowing producers to connect directly with the global marketplace, and even though provincial governments are more engaged than ever in promoting their economies abroad, what happens in Ottawa still counts.

Here it is interesting to reflect briefly on how the West's changing economic relationship with the international community might affect patterns of provincial, regional, and national identities across and within western Canada. As western Canadians turn more to face challenges of global competition and market access, will they also be turning away from the rest of Canada? Will the traditional national unity debates about Quebec's place in Canada fail to rouse even residual interest in the West? Will regional conflict between Ontario and the West increase in light of very different perspectives on greater engagement with the Asian economies? Will questions of Asian trade and market access strengthen regional identities in the West, or will these identities fall victim to increased interprovincial competition for investment, labour, and markets? Will it be all shoulders to the wheel of global competition, or will interprovincial conflict over energy policy and infrastructure erode any sense of common interest within a common region? Will western Canadians insist that the primary national economic debate should be about sustainable wealth *creation* rather than wealth *redistribution*? All of these questions tie back to our fundamental premise, that the place of the West in the global economy will shape the place of the West in Canada.

Finally, we should stress the rapid and uncertain nature of global economic change. Most of the writing for this book took place at a time when global demand was strong for the natural resources found in western Canada, and when Canada's manufacturing heartland was struggling in the face of intense international competition. Within Canada, therefore, the national economy's centre of gravity was shifting west, evidence for an ascendant West was readily available, and it was tempting to see this change of fortune as being permanent. However, the economic history of western Canada has been one of dramatic booms and equally dramatic busts, and it would be foolish to assume that economic volatility is now a thing of the past. It would be equally inappropriate to assume that the current weakness of the manufacturing sector in Canada, and for that matter in the United States, will necessarily endure, that the long-term decline of North American manufacturing is unavoidable. The Asian advantage of low wages is already in decline, and to a significant degree "in-sourcing" to North America is starting to offset the "out-sourcing" to Asia that was such an important economic feature of the last several decades. There is, then, nothing inevitable about the place of the West within the global economy, and thus within the national economy, just as there is nothing inevitable about Ontario's relative decline within the Canadian economy. This raises further questions about the role of the West within Canada. It is to these final questions that we now turn.

Notes

1   Tariffs per se are geographically neutral within the domestic economy; they have the same effect for firms in British Columbia or Ontario. The reason that the Canadian manufacturing industry came to be concentrated in Ontario was due to that province's relatively large population and its close proximity to the United States. In practice, therefore, tariff benefits including taxes and employment were concentrated in Ontario (and Quebec) through factors other than tariff policy itself. We should also keep in mind that at the onset of the National Policy in 1879 there was virtually no western Canadian industry or population to protect apart from the fur trade and Aboriginal populations.

2   For example, how much in the way of manufactured goods could a western Canadian grain farmer purchase through the sale of a given amount of wheat? For most of the twentieth century the terms of trade declined, with the consequence that farmers had to produce more and more just to maintain the same purchasing power.

6.   From Periphery to Centre

THE 2012 PASSING of former Alberta Premier Peter Lougheed drew national attention; as the *Globe and Mail* explained, "Regardless of political stripe, no matter the geographic location, tributes poured in to honour former Alberta premier Peter Lougheed" (Wingrove, Walton, and Tait 2012). While his assertions of Alberta interests and his perspectives on Canada's future were not without controversy during his time as premier—historian Doug Owram, writing for the *Toronto Star*, reported that "[o]ne Ontario cabinet minister even declared him 'a greater threat to Confederation than Quebec's René Lévesque'" (2012)—Lougheed was rightfully credited with transforming the place of Alberta *and the West* in Confederation. Here commentator Rex Murphy is worth quoting at length:

In his days as premier he personified what he was most concerned with: the New West. His presence and performance obliterated all the condescending images parts of the East held about the West and Alberta. All of the clichés, cheap putdowns and dismissals evaporated before his authority, competence and weight. . . . He presided in a period when the West and Alberta in particular were working towards some idea of their "new" presence in Confederation, when the West was claiming that it had ideas, resources and the people to join the table as an equal player . . . it was Peter Lougheed who opened the political and psychological space in which Alberta and the West have come to see themselves as full characters in the national story. In the

> genealogy of the West's rise and influence, Mr. Lougheed is the
> original force, the primary and cardinal agent. (2012)

By voicing the ideas and potentialities of the West, by bringing the region
fully to the national table, Premier Lougheed helped reshape both the
West and Canada.

In the preceding chapters, we argued along the same lines, that the
cumulative impact of incremental, widespread change across western
Canada has been transformative, that a tipping point has been reached
in how we think about western Canada and its place within the broader
Canadian community. We noted, for example, that:

- with 31 per cent of the national population, the four western provinces
  contributed 36.5 per cent of Canada's 2011 GDP, virtually on par with
  Ontario's contribution of 37.1 per cent and almost double Quebec's
  19.6 per cent contribution;
- the most rapidly growing provinces and cities are found in western
  Canada;
- with the important exception of Toronto, Canada's most ethnically
  diverse cities are in the West;
- almost 70 per cent of Canada's trade with Asian markets originates in
  western Canada, and the region attracts the bulk of Asian investment;
- two-thirds of Canada's Aboriginal population lives in the West; and
- three of the four "have provinces" are located in western Canada.

The centre of the Canadian economy, and in many ways the geopolitical
centre of the country, is moving west. This is part of the "big shift," the
New Canada described by Darrell Bricker and John Ibbitson: "It will
be more Asian and less European, more Pacific and less Atlantic. The
West will increasingly become the Centre. The failing protections for
old industries will be swept away. The great cities will grow in size and
power, while the rural and regional will further wane" (2013, 280–81).

We have also argued that it is in the West that Canada's most pressing public policy challenges of the next 20 years will be brought into
boldest relief. The need to build new urban landscapes, to forge a new
partnership with Aboriginal peoples, to ensure environmental management meets international expectations, to build bridges to the new Asian
economies, and to integrate a resource-rich, export-driven economy
into new global economic realities—all of these will play out strongly in
western Canada. Thus, while in the past western Canada was an interesting sidebar to the broader rhythms and themes of Canadian political
life, in the decades to come, understanding the West will be essential to

understanding the national community within which the West will play a larger and larger role. To again quote Bricker and Ibbitson, "western values infuse the national government. In that sense, we are all Westerners now" (2013, 103).

As Canadians living inside or outside the four western provinces attempt to come to grips with this new geopolitical reality, some important questions need to be addressed. We have already wrestled with the durability of the region's economic prosperity in the context of an uncertain continental and global economy; although we conclude that the changes of the last decade will endure, that the Canadian economy's centre of gravity will continue to shift west, there is ample room for debate on this and for that matter any economic forecast. We also need to ask whether the growing strength of western Canada will have an impact on the character of national identities and national unity. Is the West's newfound political status as part of the governing federal electoral coalition sustainable? How might provincial governments in western Canada best address the policy challenges and opportunities ahead? Is "the West" capable of being more than the sum of its provincial parts? We have considered these questions to varying degrees throughout the previous chapters, but feel it is necessary to address them more directly as we sum up our analysis.

National Identity, Federal Politics, and the West

When Premier Peter Lougheed's commitment to Canada was challenged during the constitutional turmoil of the early 1980s, when he was accused of putting Alberta first and Canada second, he argued with great passion and insight that he was a Canadian *through being an Albertan,* that the two identities were two sides of the same coin. In a similar vein, and as we argued in chapter 1, even at its height, western alienation was much more an expression of frustrated Canadian nationalism than it was an expression of disengagement from the national community.

Lougheed's observation remains true today: western Canadians identify strongly with both Canada and their provinces, as data from the 2011 Canadian Election Study (CES) demonstrate (see Figure 6.1).[1] Nor are western Canadians unique in this respect; robust national identities across Canada—with the notable exception of Quebec, although here too almost two-thirds of respondents identify with Canada—mean that nationalist appeals by political actors resonate across Canada, despite the presence of strong provincial identities. National, regional, and provincial identities happily co-exist rather than compete within the same identity space, and only in rare cases (outside Quebec) do sub-national

FIGURE 6.1 Provincial and National Identifications by Region, CES 2011

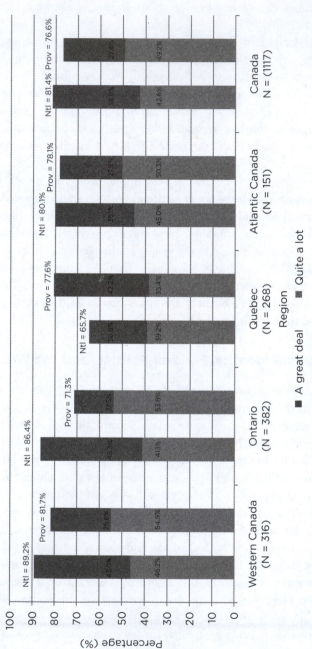

SOURCE: Canada Election Study 2011, as derived by authors. Data are weighted.

identities challenge or erode national identities. Therefore when we speak about western Canada or western Canadians, "western" is an important modifier but is also just that, a modifier; "Canada" and "Canadian" are the root terms.

However, it is not clear going forward whether national, regional, and provincial identities will continue to happily co-exist, or whether they will be thrown into competition. For example, it is still a matter of lively contention whether it is best to refer to the *Canadian oil sands*, as supporters of their development tend to do, or to the *Alberta tar sands*, as their opponents tend to do. The beneficiaries of this vast resource, and the locus of responsibility for their development and environmental mitigation, remain open to debate. A second example relates to the Port of Vancouver; should the Port best be seen as *Canada's* gateway to Asia Pacific, as the country's major export and import terminal, or as *Vancouver's* port, developed to align with the aesthetic values of metropolitan Vancouver? Whose port is it anyway, and in whose hands should responsibility for its development rest? In the provocative words of *Vancouver Sun* columnist Craig McInnes (2013), "What strains will it promote in the rest of the country if Vancouver appoints itself as an ethical troll under the bridge to foreign markets with the ability to deny passage based on local sensibilities rather than national interests?"

This brings us to another question: when political actors wrap themselves and their policy platforms in national values, when they appeal to national identities, what national values will they choose to emphasize and promote? National identity is at least partly constructed through public policy; hence the common definitions of Canada in terms of "public health care" and "peacekeeping." Until recently, Canada's "national" public policy symbols reflected primarily Liberal government policies (although again we must point out that the Charter of Rights and Freedoms was based on John Diefenbaker's 1960 Bill of Rights), but commentators have noted that Stephen Harper's Conservative government has been actively working to redefine national identity through symbols and policies drawing more from the North and military service, both past and present. Thus, the War of 1812 competes for identity space with the *Canada Health Act*, and peace-*keeping* symbols compete with more muscular peace-*making* symbols drawn from both past wars and more contemporary conflicts. Although public policy thankfully does not define national visions in their entirety, and many Canadians continue to define their country in terms of hockey, geography, and Tim Horton's coffee, public policies and the values they project still count. It is interesting to speculate, therefore, what values an unalienated and politically diverse West will bring to the national table. To return to the Port of Vancouver example, will those values tilt toward resource extraction and market access, or to recreational activities and seafront residential properties in a post-industrial society?

In chapter 1 we argued that, at different times in Canadian history, there existed in the West a national vision that ran counter to the vision that had emerged from the central Canadian historical tradition—that there were, in essence, regional differences in perceptions of what Canada is and should be. Among the threads woven into the "western vision" were notions of regional fairness and equality, and images of Canada as a cultural and linguistic melting pot, similar in spirit to the American model. Given the growing population weight of western Canada, might these alternate views of Canada enjoy greater sway? If we are correct in describing regional discontent, even western alienation, as a sense of frustrated Canadian nationalism, then what are the values left on the table when frustration wanes? What is the western vision beyond a historically rooted, pervasive sense of injustice?

In answer to this question, we must return to one of the ironies of Canadian constitutional politics. As detailed in chapter 1, despite the fact that the major constitutional debates over the past half-century addressed Quebec concerns and the national unity threat of Quebecois nationalism, the end result has been constitutional change that reflected western Canadian more than Quebec constitutional ideals. Thus, while specific federal policies may be critiqued (rightly or wrongly) as being regionally unfair, the constitutional "rules of the game" are not weighted against the West (with the notable exception of Senate representation). If there is a regional bias against the West, it is most evident in public policy. Moving forward, be it with the Conservative government of the day or some future NDP, Liberal, or NDP-Liberal government, it is possible that there will be a growing shift toward less partisan federal policy decision-making on issues of potential regional contention. We may, for example, see more use of "delegated decision-making," such as was used in the October 2011 awarding of shipbuilding contracts, whereby shipyard contracts were awarded to Halifax and Vancouver and not to a Quebec-based shipyard. There have also been calls for the equalization formula to be set by a nonpartisan committee. The willingness of federal governments to use nonpartisan commissions to determine policy will undoubtedly vary by the temperature of the particular policy "potato," and it can be argued that the use of such unelected, not-publicly-accountable commissions is problematic on democratic grounds. Nonetheless, we may see a willingness for more expansive decision-making forums in policy areas such as Aboriginal affairs where partisanship and ideology provide limited guidance.

This brings us to another consideration, and that is the degree to which western Canada's influence on national policy is primarily a function of contemporary partisan configurations, ones that are always subject to change. For instance, much ado has been made about the West's newfound status as part of the governing electoral coalition. For the first time in Canadian history, a majority federal government was elected in 2011 through the support of Ontario and the western provinces, and with small, inconsequential support from Quebec. In the view of some, this marks a fundamental shift, reflecting both the rise of western Canadian political might and the decline of Quebec's predominance in federal politics. In the view of others, the West–Ontario electoral coalition is bound to be temporary. The West has been part of governing electoral coalitions in the past, only to be returned to the opposition benches: most recently, we must highlight the Mulroney government's electoral support from the West and Quebec, the aftermath of which left both regions in opposition, with the West voting heavily for the Reform Party and Quebec for the Bloc Québécois in the 1993 general election.

What, then, is the sustainability of the West's newfound central role in the national conversation; is it a flash in the pan or an enduring structural change? While political forecasting is more perilous than weather or economic forecasting, our argument throughout the book has been that western Canada is no longer the hinterland, and that it will not return to the periphery when the Conservatives eventually lose power. There have been significant structural changes that mean that the "inness" of the West goes beyond the contemporary partisan configuration and can be expected to survive the inevitable partisan reconfiguration, that for any party the road to national power will run through the West.

On what basis do we make this bold assertion? Here we point to population change, and more specifically to the distribution of seats in the House of Commons. A new "representational order" will be in effect as of April 2014 (Elections Canada, n.d.). In subsequent elections until the next decennial census, 104 of Canada's 338 House seats will be in western Canada (42 in British Columbia, 34 in Alberta, 14 each in Saskatchewan and Manitoba), 121 in Ontario, 78 in Quebec, 32 in Atlantic Canada (11 in Nova Scotia, 10 in New Brunswick, 7 in Newfoundland and Labrador, and 4 in Prince Edward Island), and 3 in the North (one for each territory). Given these numbers, and the fact that a majority government would require a party (or coalition of parties, should Canadians decide to test those waters) to hold 170 or more seats, it is in the interest of all federal parties to work to build their western support.

As Ibbitson explains: "Today, Quebec is far less central to the national agenda. . . . The West has replaced Quebec as the n in the equation Ontario plus n equals a majority government" (2012). All parties can be expected to see the West, or at least parts of the West, as a key component of future winning coalitions. Indeed, it has been argued that the NDP are seeking to build a Quebec–BC electoral coalition; according to Eric Grenier, who runs the popular ThreeHundredEight.com website, "With continued dominance in Quebec, B.C. could be the second plank of an NDP election victory in 2015" (2012). Similarly, the Liberals have long been striving to regain electoral support in western Canada, and such efforts are unlikely to disappear. Quite apart from opposition by Thomas Mulcair, there are not enough Quebec seats alone to propel Justin Trudeau into national office.

In short, there are simply too many House of Commons seats in the region for federal politicians to ignore western Canada. However, the amount of political wooing directed at the individual western provinces will most certainly differ. We noted in chapter 1 that the overall electoral importance of "the West" was only modestly enhanced by the *Fair Representation Act*'s redistribution formula due to the existing electoral overrepresentation of Manitoba and Saskatchewan. It is British Columbia and Alberta where seats were gained, and it is those two provinces that stand to attract the most intense courtship. British Columbia, with its 42 seats and more ideologically diverse population, will be vigorously contested, while Alberta, despite its 34 seats, will receive less attention. As columnist Don Martin argues,

> The prism view of decision-making in Ottawa, even under the reign of Calgary MP Stephen Harper, fractures into light shining on Quebec, Ontario and B.C., in that order. Until Alberta voters become less predictable, this will never change. The bluest of the provinces will always be ignored as a dead zone by any Liberal government and taken for granted as an electoral birthright by Conservatives. (2010)

Thus, while the West made its way "in" through regional bloc voting, its ongoing political importance would be strengthened through greater partisan diversity and thereby a more competitive environment.

It should also be noted that in the minds of Canadian voters and in the electoral calculations of political parties, not all seats are the same, and that greater priority may be placed on shoring up Quebec representation than numbers alone may suggest. A December 2012 national survey found that most Canadians perceive the Quebec question as the most serious regional conflict in the country (Abacus Data 2012). Eighty per cent of Canadians rated the conflict between Quebec and the rest of Canada as very or somewhat serious compared with 42 per cent for "Western Canada versus Eastern Canada," 45 per cent for "Alberta versus the rest of Canada," and 26 per cent for "British Columbia versus Alberta." According to Abacus Data CEO David Coletto,

> A large majority of Canadians across the country, including in
> Quebec, believe that the Quebec question will be the greater
> problem for Canadian national unity over the next 20 years
> than conflict between eastern and western Canada. While many
> consider conflict between Alberta and the rest of Canada as
> serious, the level of concern is still nowhere near that of issues
> around Quebec. (Abacus Data 2012)

Given this reality, political support from Quebec may continue to com-
mand greater attention than the province's waning demographic strength
would predict, although minimal Quebec representation in the post-
2011 federal government did not trigger a great deal of hand-wringing
either inside or outside Quebec.

Western Provincial Governments and the Future of Canada

While much attention has been given to the potential impact of the West
within the federal government, it is important to stress that the region's
capacity to shape national policy is not limited to its representation in
Ottawa. We began this chapter by discussing Peter Lougheed's influence
on reshaping the federation; the West's impact on Canadian federalism
will also be felt through federal–provincial relations, through provincial–
territorial relations (be it within the Council of the Federation or in
other forums), or through provincial policy. The actions and positions
of the western provincial governments could have profound impact on
the evolving nature of Canadian federalism, and it is to that topic that
we now turn.

The West's growing population and its strong contributions to the
national economy have not only increased the region's role in Canada,
but also have created specific policy needs. What may be striking to
some readers is that while we see these as being of national importance,
we do not necessarily call for a national or federal response. As previously discussed, due to the jurisdictional division of powers and the shift
in the scope of federal engagement in provincial policy since the 1990s,
it is provincial governments who have both the authority and capacity
to respond to many of these policy issues; there is ample room for policy leadership and policy coordination through and among provincial
governments. To take but one example, the position of the BC government toward pipeline development, and the more general movement of
resources through BC ports, could well be decisive.

As the four western provincial governments move forward, it is an
open question as to whether they should deliberately seek to act "as

a region"—that is, if it makes both strategic and policy sense to work together. As we explained in chapter 4, the West's actions as a political region over time have varied considerably depending upon the interests of provincial political actors. Although we believe that "the West" is more than the sum of its provincial parts, we equally feel that differences within the West cannot be glossed over. Certainly this is emphatically the case when it comes to disputes over Asian market access for resource producers across the region.

Writing a decade ago, we noted an economic and demographic "east-west" divide within western Canada, with British Columbia and Alberta enjoying stronger population and economic growth than Saskatchewan and Manitoba (Gibbins and Berdahl 2003). This divide has lessened over the decade: Saskatchewan has (to the surprise of many) emerged as one of Canada's economic leaders, with a booming population, and Manitoba too is enjoying a resurgence. While British Columbia and Alberta remain considerably larger than Saskatchewan and Manitoba, all four provinces enjoy relatively strong growth and prosperity. At the same time, important barriers may stand in the way of greater regional cooperation. We noted the institutional barriers in chapter 4, and will not elaborate on those here, if for no other reason than the fact that if the four western provinces wished to create a robust regional institutional home, they could do so. Instead, we will point to two barriers that may prove particularly cumbersome.

The first, somewhat esoteric barrier lies in identities. While almost all definitions of "the West" include Alberta and Saskatchewan, there is less consensus on the inclusion of British Columbia and Manitoba. With respect to British Columbia, the province has always stood somewhat apart in the region, with the Rocky Mountains presenting both a physical and psychological divide. BC politics has often looked outward (to the United States, to the Pacific Rim) rather than inward (to the region, to Canada), and while western-based political parties (Social Credit, the Reform Party, the Canadian Alliance) enjoyed considerable success in British Columbia, the fact remains that the western critique of Canadian nationalism emerged primarily from the prairie provinces. Thus, in many respects British Columbia fits uneasily within the broader region. Manitoba is more of a puzzle. Although sharing considerable political and economic history with Saskatchewan and Alberta, Manitoba often seems to have one foot firmly planted in the West, but not both; it is the most eastern of the western provinces in both geographic and attitudinal terms while still retaining western outlooks that clearly delineate Manitoba and Ontario. The extent to which Manitobans see their province as an integral part of the "New West" may hinge on whether

Manitoba eventually joints the New West Partnership, and whether the NWP provides institutional coherence and leadership for the region.

The second, and more structural barrier to the western provinces taking a more regional approach lies with varying and potentially conflicting interests. There are many areas in which the four provinces share strong interests (urbanization, labour supply, and Aboriginal peoples, to name just three), but there are areas of important difference. Take, for example, the issue of energy policy. All four western provinces are strong energy producers and have considerable interest in energy policy. Three of the four have robust coal industries (British Columbia, Alberta, and Saskatchewan), three of the four (British Columbia, Alberta, and Saskatchewan) are major oil and/or gas producers (along with the small southwestern corner of Manitoba), and two of the four (British Columbia and Manitoba) are hydro-producing provinces. However, a shared stake in energy policy does not necessarily lead to shared interests, as the tension between Alberta and British Columbia with respect to pipeline access to the west coast so vividly demonstrates. Differing energy portfolios can create important differences on energy policy, climate change policy, and environmental policy—even before the ideological differences among provincial governments are factored in. Such structural factors may limit the range of policy areas open for strategic regional partnerships. This is the paradox of energy resources across the West; they bring the region together while at the same time potentially rendering it asunder.

While recognizing these important barriers, we nevertheless suggest that there remains considerable opportunity for strategic partnerships among the western provinces. Further, just as interprovincial partnerships within the West are likely to become more important in the future, so too are strategic partnerships with communities and interests outside the region.[2] The West is not an island unto itself within Canada or within the continental and global economies, and a number of key partnership possibilities come to mind:

- First Nations. There is a pressing need for strategic partnerships with First Nations communities across the West. Resource and human capital development, tourism, and environmental protection hinge on achieving an effective intergovernmental relationship within which common interests can be pursued and conflicts addressed. This may take some time and will ultimately be conditional on the settlement of land claims and the full institutionalization of First Nations governments. Still, it is a distant goal toward which western Canada can begin to move, indeed must begin to move as a regional community. It is difficult to

see how the global positioning of a resource-rich regional economy can
be secured without the full and constructive engagement of Aboriginal
peoples.

- The North. Potential energy developments in the northern territories,
  including the possible Mackenzie Valley pipeline, pipeline connections
  to Alaskan natural gas fields, and energy plays in the Arctic Ocean,
  could all have a substantial economic impact on the prosperity of the
  western provinces. In fact, the potential southern impact may even
  exceed that on the northern territories themselves. A great deal of
  the engineering work, transportation activity, purchase of materials
  and equipment, and labour pool will come from the provinces, and a
  great deal of the financial benefits will stick to the south. For example,
  Edmonton's role as the gateway to the North affords the city, and indirectly the province, tremendous opportunities. There is, then, great complementarity between the economic interests of the North and West, and
  managing this complementarity will be an important political task. In
  this way, the inclusion of the northern premiers in the Western Premiers'
  Conference may be particularly beneficial.
- Atlantic Canada. Energy developments off the coasts of Newfoundland
  and Labrador and Nova Scotia, and potentially huge natural gas
  deposits in New Brunswick, also open up new possibilities for strategic
  regional partnerships. There is a shared interest in protecting provincial
  jurisdiction over, and ownership of, natural resources, and a shared
  interest in national policies designed to foster rather than impair a
  robust Canadian energy sector. Atlantic ports and refineries may provide outlets for western oil producers struggling for American and
  Asian markets (Saint John, New Brunswick, is closer by sea to India
  than is Vancouver). Although opportunities for regional alliances have
  seldom been explored in the past, they may become more important
  in the future. It should be noted, however, that the West's historical
  relationship with Atlantic Canada has been far from smooth. Atlantic
  Canadians often saw western Canadian growth as coming at the
  expense of their own region, and western Canadian perspectives on the
  national community often stopped at "Central Canada." Just as western Canadians have complained that "national" visions too frequently
  ignore the West, national visions emerging from the West too often pay
  only glancing attention to Atlantic Canada. If effective strategic partnerships are to evolve, broader national visions may be needed on both
  sides of the continent.
- Ontario. Of particular importance to the western provinces moving forward is the complex and too-often contentious relationship
  with Ontario. Although there have been and are very real regional

conflicts—the NEP, for example, had a near-catastrophic impact on the West while providing lower energy prices for Ontario consumers (hence the popular 1980s Alberta bumper sticker, "Let the Eastern Bastards Freeze in the Dark"), and the support for a national securities regulator is much stronger in Ontario than it is in western Canada—there are also shared interests. Ontario and the West remain Canada's economic and demographic growth poles, and both regions are struggling for global positioning in a new economic order. Hopefully potential policy conflicts over such issues as equalization, carbon pricing and immigration can be minimized through constructive intergovernmental relations.

- Quebec. As we have pointed out in previous chapters, Quebec and the West have often been at loggerheads with respect to national visions and the redistributive impact of federal programs. Quebec has been the "in" while the West has been the counterpoint "out." However, common ground is much less elusive than is commonly thought. The possibility of a more decentralized federal state, and greater provincial autonomy with respect to social policy, could enjoy broad support in both regions. Current tensions over energy and climate policies may be reduced if Quebec moves to develop newly found hydrocarbon fields in the province, and if repurposed pipelines could provide western Canadian feedstock to Quebec refineries. Quebec's relative success in creating innovative partnerships with Aboriginal peoples provides policy examples upon which provincial governments in the West might build.

- The United States. State governments in the American northwest open up another venue for strategic partnerships. There has been a long history of bilateral relationships between state and provincial governments in the western part of the continent. While in the past those relationships tended to be informal, irregular, and at a modest level in the political hierarchy, there are signs today that they are becoming more regular. Broader forums for interaction include the Pacific North-West Economic Region (PNWER) that incorporates Alaska, Alberta, British Columbia, Idaho, Montana, the Northwest Territories, Oregon, Saskatchewan, Washington and the Yukon, and which provides a forum for the discussion of both economic issues common to the region and regional collaboration. There has also been considerable if more abstract discussion of Cascadia, a bio-region along the western side of the Coastal range that includes at the very least the shared watershed environments of British Columbia and Washington, and at times is extended conceptually from northern California to Alaska. These initiatives provide an initial forum within which to explore regional partnerships across state, provincial, and international borders. Although such partnerships are unlikely to approach the economic importance of regional partnerships in the European Union, they should not be ignored. With the growing volume of north-south trade and the relative decline of east-west trade, regional organizations spanning the international border will take on more weight.

To be certain, advancing strategic partnerships only works when all parties feel their interests are being advanced. Cooperative action must make sense for all partners, and at the end of the day provincial governments are responsible to their own electorates who will evaluate them based on the provincial economy and quality of life, among other factors. The challenge for the western Canadian governments, therefore, is to establish foundational relationships that allow for partnerships and cooperation when such opportunities present themselves.

In the past, much of the regional glue for western Canada was (unintentionally) provided by the Government of Canada; opposition to federal policies and a shared sense of exclusion from the centres of economic, political, and cultural power knit together a diverse regional community. Now that the West is much closer to these centres of power, and now that federal policy is better aligned with western Canadian interests and aspirations, it remains to be seen whether the potential for cooperation within the region, and between the West and other regions, will provide an equally powerful glue. It is entirely possible that, as the West moves from periphery to centre, it will weaken as a *regional* community.

Conclusion

The future prosperity of Canada is inextricably tied to the future of the West. As the preceding chapters have shown, the West is rich in assets that will continue to benefit Canada—an energetic and diverse population, myriad natural resources, a strong economy, and a long history of multiculturalism, hard work, and innovation. Western Canada is a region marked by great promise and even greater aspirations. For these reasons, western visions must be part of the national vision going forward. In the past, regional discontent was fanned by an alternative national vision that found little traction outside the West, particularly as Canadians struggled to come to grips with the nationalist movement in Quebec. Today, that alternative vision is finding greater traction.

Western Canada, moreover, will cast into bold relief an existential question for all Canadians: what will happen to a resource-rich, export-driven economy when the resources run out or, more likely, when markets weaken in the face of technological change and intensifying international competition? In the words of economist Todd Hirsch:

"The worrying question used to be: What if we run out of oil? That's been answered. We will never, ever run out of oil. Now the more daunting question is: What if we can't transport our oil to the buyers? Or worse, what if they don't need our oil anymore?" (2013).

Going forward, what will be Canada's niche in the global economy? We have argued that recent changes within the Canadian economy are likely to be structural and enduring, but this does not mean that Canadians either inside or outside the West will necessarily be well-served by those changes. Can we prosper in the years to come, or do all Canadians face wrenching changes to the economic status quo? To return to the question posed indirectly by Thomas Mulcair in chapter 3, will the West be the new motor of the Canadian economy or will it be sand in the gears of Canada's economic transformation?

Here we would suggest that western Canada serves as the canary in Canada's economic mine shaft. If western Canadians are able to create a successful model for a knowledge-based yet resource dependent regional economy thoroughly embedded in the global economy, the lessons learned will be Canadian lessons. As we have argued throughout, the challenges faced by western Canada in a topsy-turvy global economy are not unique to the region. Volatile international prices, growing economic competition, demographic change, market access and international trade agreements, labour shortages, Aboriginal aspirations, growing environmental pressures with respect to how we produce, consume, and live, and dependency on American markets are all *Canadian* realities that no region escapes; they just seem more urgent, more acute in the West. Yes, the regional economy in western Canada is different, but many of the differences are of degree, not kind. Thus if we "get it right" in the West, we stand a good chance of getting it right nationally.

We have argued throughout that western Canadians, fed by immigration and focused on global markets, have always been outward looking. To use the clichés of the day, there has always been a need to think big, to think outside the regional and even Canadian box. In this respect, little will change in the years ahead. Western Canadians, and in particular resource producers, have a huge task in establishing the West's brand within the international marketplace and investment community. The regional brand brings together not only where we live but also how we live, what we produce and how we produce it, and all of this is coming under growing international scrutiny in a rapidly globalizing environment. Fortunately, the West has many advantages from which to construct a strong regional brand, including but by no means limited to an often stunning geography—and lots of it!—and an immense natural resource endowment. Western Canadians also benefit greatly from the Canadian brand and its demonstrated albeit not unshakeable global reputation. Still, it remains to be seen what values will be reflected in the western Canadian brand, and the Canadian brand with which it is inescapably connected. Will the values forged through generations of frontier experience and political protest serve the region, and Canada, well going forward?

Writing over 40 years ago, historian J.M.S. Careless suggested a vision for Canada: "What has been sought and to some degree achieved is not really unification or consolidation, but the articulation of regional patterns in one transcontinental state" (1969, 9). We would suggest that this vision—"the articulation of regional patterns in one transcontinental state"—remains as important to Canada today as it did in the past. At the time Careless wrote, western Canada was just beginning to reassert itself on the national stage and, with the outburst of regional discontent and western alienation, the West was seen as a problem to be solved. Today, it is an opportunity to be seized.

Notes

1 CES mail back survey respondents were asked, "How much do you identify with each of the following: your neighbourhood, your city/town, your province, Canada, the world?" Response options included "a great deal," "quite a lot," "not very much," and "none at all." As these questions were part of the CES mail back survey, which had a smaller sample sizes, we present these data on a regional basis; weighted sample sizes for the four Atlantic and three prairie provinces are less than 100 per province, making it difficult to generalize about specific provinces.

2 We would like to thank Peter Lougheed and Preston Manning for directing our thoughts in this direction.

Bibliography

Abacus Data. 2012. *News Release: Poll: Conflict between Quebec and the Rest of Canada Considered More Serious than Other Regional Conflicts in Canada.* http://www.abacusdata.ca (December 19, 2012).

Abbott, Michael, and Charles Beach. 2011. "Working Paper No. 81—Immigrant Earnings Differences across Admission Categories and Landing Cohorts in Canada." *Canadian Labour Market and Skills Researcher Network.* Forthcoming.

Abma, Derek. 2011. "Western Canadian Cities to See Strongest Economic Growth: Report." *Financial Post,* May 5. http://business.financialpost.com/2011/05/05/western-canadian-cities-to-see-strongest-economic-growth-report/ (May 26, 2013).

Abma, Derek. 2012. "Some Provinces Suffering Because of Oil Sands Prosperity: Thomas Mulcair." *National Post,* May 7. http://news.nationalpost.com/2012/05/05/some-provinces-suffering-because-of-oil-sands-prosperity-ndps-thomas-mulcair/ (May 26, 2013).

Abrams, Dominic, and Michael A. Hogg, eds. 1999. *Social Identity and Social Cognition.* Oxford: Blackwell Publishers.

Akin, David. 2012. "Quebec, Canada Divide Deepens." *Toronto Sun,* August 14. http://www.torontosun.com/2012/08/14/divide-deepens-between-quebec-and-rest-of-canada (August 26, 2013).

Alberta, British Columbia, and Saskatchewan. 2010a. *News Release: Saskatchewan, Alberta and BC Launch New West Partnership. 30 April.*

Alberta, British Columbia, and Saskatchewan. 2010b. *News Release: Premiers Lead New West Partnership Asian Trade Mission.*

Alberta, British Columbia, and Saskatchewan. 2010c. *New West Partnership Backgrounder.* http://www.gov.sk.ca/nwp (May 26, 2013).

Alberta, British Columbia, and Saskatchewan. 2010d. *New West Partnership Agreement.* http://www.gov.sk.ca/nwp (May 26, 2013).

Alberta Federation of Labour. 2010. "Western Premiers Ink Deal to Tumble Trade
    Barriers: Provinces to Pool Drug Purchases, International Marketing Plans."
    AFL in the News, May 1. http://www.afl.org/index.php/AFL-in-the-News/
    western-premiers-ink-deal-to-tumble-trade-barriers-provinces-to-pool-drug-
    purchases-intl-marketing-plans.html (May 26, 2013).
Allen, Richard. 1973. *A Region of the Mind.* Regina: Canadian Plains Study Centre.
Anderson, Cameron. 2010. "Regional Heterogeneity and Policy Preferences in
    Canada: 1979–2006." *Regional & Federal Studies* 20 (4–5): 447–68. http://
    dx.doi.org/10.1080/13597566.2010.523620.
Banerjee, Robin, and William Robson. 2009. "Faster, Younger, Richer? The Fond
    Hope and Sobering Reality of Immigration's Impact on Canada's Demographic
    and Economic Future." *C.D. Howe Institute Commentary* 291: 1–24.
Barman, Jean. 1993. *The West Beyond the West: A History of British Columbia.*
    Toronto: University of Toronto Press.
Basavarajappa, K.G., and Bali Ram. 2008. "Table A2–14 Population of Canada, By
    Province, Census Dates, 1851 to 1976." *Statistics Canada.* October 22. http://
    www5.statcan.gc.ca/access_acces/archive.action?l=eng&loc=A2_14-eng.csv
    (May 26, 2013).
Bashevkin, Sylvia. 1991. *True Patriot Love: The Politics of Canadian Nationalism.*
    Toronto: Oxford University Press.
Beaujot, Roderic, and Don Kerr. 2004. *Population Change in Canada.* 2nd ed. Don
    Mills, ON: Oxford University Press.
Béland, Daniel, and André Lecours. 2008. *Nationalism and Social Policy: The
    Politics of Territorial Solidarity.* Oxford: Oxford University Press. http://dx.doi.
    org/10.1093/acprof:oso/9780199546848.001.0001.
Béland, Daniel, and André Lecours. 2011. "The Ideational Dimension of Federalism:
    The 'Australian Model' and the Politics of Equalisation in Canada." *Australian
    Journal of Political Science* 46 (2): 199–212. http://dx.doi.org/10.1080/103611
    46.2011.567974.
Béland, Daniel, and André Lecours. 2012. *Equalization at Arm's Length.* Toronto:
    Mowatt Centre for Policy Innovation.
Bell, David, and Lorne Tepperman. 1979. *The Roots of Disunity: A Look at
    Canadian Political Culture.* Toronto: McClelland and Stewart.
Bell, David. 1992. *The Roots of Disunity.* Toronto: Oxford University Press.
Bennett, Dean. 2012. "Justin Trudeau to Face Ghosts of Western Alienation in Bid
    for Liberal Crown." *The Canadian Press,* October 3. http://infotel.ca/newsitem/
    Liberal-Leadership-Trudeau-West/CP20321391 (October 3, 2012).
Berdahl, Loleen. 2004. *Regional Distinctions: An Analysis of the Looking West 2004
    Survey.* Calgary: Canada West Foundation.
Berdahl, Loleen. 2006. *Political Identities in Western Canada: An Analysis of the
    Looking West 2006 Survey.* Calgary: Canada West Foundation.
Berdahl, Loleen. 2011. "Region-building: Western Canadian Joint Cabinet Meetings
    in the 2000s." *Canadian Public Administration* 54 (2): 255–75. http://dx.doi.
    org/10.1111/j.1754-7121.2011.00173.x.
Berdahl, Loleen. 2013. "(Sub)National Economic Union: Institutions, Ideas, and
    Internal Trade Policy in Canada." *Publius: The Journal of Federalism* 43 (2):
    275–96. http://dx.doi.org/10.1093/publius/pjs036.
Beyle, Thad L. 1974. "New Directions in Interstate Relations." *Annals of the
    American Academy of Political and Social Science* 416 (1): 108–19. http://
    dx.doi.org/10.1177/000271627441600111.
Bilodeau, Antoine, Stephen White, and Neil Nevitte. 2010. "The Development of
    Dual Loyalties: Immigrants' Integration to Canadian Regional Dynamics."
    Canadian Journal of Political Science 43 (3): 515–44. http://dx.doi.org/10.1017/
    S0008423910000600.

Blake, Donald. 1972. "The Measurement of Regionalism in Canadian Voting Patterns." *Canadian Journal of Political Science* 5 (1): 55–81. http://dx.doi.org/10.1017/S0008423900027359.

BMO Economics. 2012a. "News Release: Western Canada Driving Canadian Economic Growth." http://newsroom.bmo.com/press-releases/bmo-economics-western-canada-driving-canadian-eco-tsx-bmo-201205030787395001 (May 26, 2013).

BMO Economics. 2012b. "Provincial Monitor." http://www.bmonesbittburns.com/economics/monitor/201210/monitor.pdf (May 26, 2013).

Bolleyer, Nicole. 2006. "Federal Dynamics in Canada, the United States, and Switzerland: How Substates' Internal Organization Affects Intergovernmental Relations." *Publius: The Journal of Federalism* 36 (4): 471–502. http://dx.doi.org/10.1093/publius/pjl003.

Bolleyer, Nicole. 2009. *Intergovernmental Cooperation: Rational Choices in Federal Systems and Beyond.* New York: Oxford University Press. http://dx.doi.org/10.1093/acprof:oso/9780199570607.001.0001.

Boswell, Randy. 2012. "Census: Canada's Growth Fastest in G8 as Population Hits 33.5 Million." 8 February. http://news.nationalpost.com/2012/02/08/canada-census-2011-canadas-leads-g8-in-growth-population-hits-33-5-million/http://www.canada.com/technology/Census+Canada+growth+fastest+population+hits+million/6119664/story.html (June 20, 2012).

Breton, Raymond. 1981. "Regionalism in Canada" In *Regionalism and Supranationalism,* ed. David Cameron, 57–79. Montreal: The Institute for Research on Public Policy.

Bricker, Darrell, and John Ibbitson. 2013. *The Big Shift: The Seismic Change in Canadian Politics, Business and Culture and What It Means for Our Future.* Toronto: HarperCollins.

Brodie, Janine. 1990. *The Political Economy of Canadian Regionalism.* Toronto: Harcourt Brace.

Brodie, Janine. 2003. "On Being Canadian." In *Reinventing Canada: Politics of the 21st Century,* ed. Janine Brodie and Linda Trimble, 18–31. Toronto: Prentice Hall.

Calgary Herald. 2001. "What the West Wants." January 27, OS6.

Cameron, David, and Richard Simeon. 2002. "Intergovernmental Relations in Canada: The Emergence of Collaborative Federalism." *Publius: The Journal of Federalism* 32 (2): 49–71. http://dx.doi.org/10.1093/oxfordjournals.pubjof.a004947.

Campbell, David. 2011. "The Demographic Tsunami Will Hit Atlantic Canada First." *Globe and Mail,* November 8. http://www.theglobeandmail.com/report-on-business/economy/economy-lab/the-demographic-tsunami-will-hit-atlantic-canada-first/article619021/#dashboard/follows/ (June 20, 2012).

Campbell, Robert, and Leslie A. Pal. 1989. *The Real World of Canadian Politics: Cases in Process and Policy.* Peterborough, ON: Broadview Press.

Campion-Smith, Bruce. 2012. "2011 Canada Census: Growth Out West Outpacing Ontario." *Toronto Star,* February 8. http://www.thestar.com/news/canada/2012/02/08/2011_canada_census_growth_out_west_outpacing_ontario.html (June 18, 2012).

Canada. 2012a. "Booming Opportunity = Investor Profitability." October 15. http://investincanada.gc.ca/eng/ (October 15, 2012).

Canada. 2012b. "Organization Profile–Atlantic Canada Opportunities." December 20. http://www.appointments.gc.ca/prflOrg.asp?OrgID=ACB&lang=eng (December 20, 2012).

Canadian Broadcasting Corporation News (CBC). 2011. "Kenney Lauds Provinces' Immigration Success." November 21. http://www.cbc.ca/news/politics/story/2011/11/21/pol-immigration-kenney-skilled.html (May 26, 2013).

Canadian Broadcasting Corporation News (CBC). 2012. "Canadian Census
    Shows People Moving West." February 8. http://www.cbc.ca/news/canada/
    story/2012/02/08/census-2011-main.html (June 18, 2012).
Careless, J.M.S. 1969. "'Limited Identities' in Canada." *Canadian Historical Review*
    50: 1–10.
Carter, Tom, Manish Pandey, and James Townsend. 2010. "The Manitoba Provincial
    Nominee Program." *IRPP Study* 74: 1–44.
Cernetig, Miro. 2010. "BC, Alberta and Saskatchewan Premiers Sell 'the New West'
    to the World." *Vancouver Sun*, May 14.
Chang, Gordon G. 2011. *The Coming Collapse of China*. New York: Random House.
Citizenship and Immigration Canada. 2010. "Canada—Permanent Residents by
    Province or Territory and Category. Statistics—Facts and Figures—Immigration
    Overview: Permanent and Temporary Residents." http://www.cic.gc.ca/english/
    resources/statistics/menu-fact.asp (May 26, 2013).
Citizenship and Immigration Canada. 2012. "Consultations on Immigration Levels
    for 2012 and Beyond: Report of Findings." http://www.cic.gc.ca/english/pdf/
    pub/consultations-imm-levels.pdf (May 26, 2013).
Clarke, Harold, Jon Pammett, and Marianne Stewart. 2002. "The Forest for the
    Trees: Regional (Dis)Similarities in Canadian Political Culture." In *Regionalism
    and Party Politics*, ed. Lisa Young and Keith Archer, 43–76. Don Mills, ON:
    Oxford University Press.
Conference Board of Canada. 2012. "News Release: Provincial Economics in for a
    Bumpy Ride in the Short Term." July 27. http://www.conferenceboard.ca/press/
    newsrelease/12-07-27/provincial_economies_in_for_a_bumpy_ride_in_the_
    short_term.aspx (July 27, 2012).
Conrad, Margaret. 1993. "'The 1950's': The Decade of Development." In *The
    Atlantic Provinces in Confederation*, ed. E.R. Forbes and D.A. Muise, 382–420.
    Toronto: University of Toronto Press.
Cooper, Barry. 2002. "Regionalism, Political Culture, and Canadian Political
    Myths." In *Regionalism and Party Politics*, ed. Lisa Young and Keith Archer,
    92–112. Don Mills, ON: Oxford University Press.
Copeland, Brian R. 2008. "Is There a Case for Trade and Investment Promotion
    Policy?" In *Trade Policy Research*, ed. Dan Ciuriak, 1–64. Ottawa: Foreign
    Affairs and International Trade Canada.
Creighton, Donald. 1980. *The Passionate Observer: Selected Writings*. Toronto:
    McClelland and Stewart.
Decloet, Derek. 2012. "Compared to Alberta, Ontario Are the Real Conservatives."
    Globe and Mail, September 6. http://www.theglobeandmail.com/report-on-
    business/rob-magazine/compared-to-alberta-ontario-are-the-real-conservatives/
    article4096679/#dashboard/follows/ (September 6, 2012).
Dennison, Donald G. 2005. "Intergovernmental Mechanisms: What Have We
    Learned? Retrospective on the Conduct of Intergovernmental Relations: Review
    of Machinery and Processes of Relations among Governments in Canada, and
    Their Evolution Over the Years." Presented at Looking Backward, Thinking
    Forward Conference for the Institute of Intergovernmental Relations at Queen's
    University, Kingston, Ontario.
DeSouza, Mike. 2011. "Tory Bill Adds 30 New MPs to House of Commons."
    National Post, October 27. http://news.nationalpost.com/2011/10/27/tory-bill-
    would-add-30-new-mps-to-house-of-commons/ (October 27, 2011).
Dupré, J. Stefan. 1988. "Reflections on the Workability of Executive Federalism." In
    Perspectives on Canadian Federalism, ed. R.D. Olling and M.W. Westmacott,
    233–56. Scarborough, ON: Prentice-Hall Canada.
Dupuis, Jean. 2011. *Federal Regional Economic Development Organizations:
    Background Paper*. Ottawa: Library of Parliament.

Edmonston, Barry, and Eric Fong. 2011. "Introduction." In *The Changing Canadian Population*, ed. Barry Edmonston and Eric Fong, 3–19. Montreal: McGill-Queen's University Press.

Elections Canada. No date. "Timeline for the Redistribution of Federal Election Districts." http://www.elections.ca/content.aspx?section=res&dir=cir/red/over&document=index&lang=e (November 16, 2012).

Elkins, David J., and Richard Simeon. 1980. *Small Worlds: Provinces and Parties in Canadian Political Life*. Toronto: Methuen.

Emery, J.C. Herbert, and Ronald D. Kneebone. 2003. "Should Alberta and Saskatchewan Unite? Examining Proposals for Closer Co-Operation—From Maintaining the Status Quo to Political Union." *C.D. Howe Institute Commentary*, No. 190 (November).

Fekete, Jason. 2011. "Western Canada Can 'Breathe a Lot Easier'; Harper Maps Out Tory Majority." *Calgary Herald*, May 4. http://www2.canada.com/calgaryherald/news/story.html?id=581ab4a6-8764-44fd-b897-4382f026c226&p=2 (August 26, 2013).

Ferley, Paul, Robert Hogue, and Laura Cooper. 2013. *RBC Economics: Provincial Outlook March 2013*. http://www.rbc.com/newsroom/pdf/provfcst-03-2013.pdf (October 31, 2013).

Finbow, Robert. 2004. "Atlantic Canada in the Twenty-First Century: Prospects for Reggional Integration." In *Regionalism in a Global Society: Persistence and Change in Atlantic Canada*, ed. Charles S. Colgan and Stephen G. Tomblin, 149–70. Toronto: University of Toronto Press.

Foot, David, and Daniel Stoffman. 1998. *Boom, Bust and Echo 2000*. Toronto: Macfarlane Walter & Ross.

Fowke, Vernon C. 1957. *The National Policy and the Wheat Economy*. Toronto: University of Toronto Press.

Fox, Lisa, and Robert Roach. 2003. *Good Neighbours: An Inventory of Interprovincial Cooperation in the West, 1990–2002*. Calgary: Canada West Foundation.

Friesen, Gerald. 1984. *The Canadian Prairies: A History*. Toronto: University of Toronto Press.

Friesen, Joe. 2012. "Immigrant Drop Imperils Ontario Economy." *Globe and Mail*, February 6. http://www.theglobeandmail.com/news/politics/immigrant-drop-imperils-ontario-economy/article4197576/#dashboard/follows/ (June 22, 2012).

Friesen, Joe, and Bill Curry. 2012. "Canada's Future is in the West: 2011 Census." *Globe and Mail*, February 8. http://www.theglobeandmail.com/news/natio-nal/canadas-future-is-in-the-west-2011-census/article544556/ (June 18, 2012).

Friesen, Joe, and Josh Wingrove. 2012. "Ontario Cedes Centre Stage to a Thriving West, Census Shows." *Globe and Mail*, September 6. http://m.theglobeandmail.com/news/national/ontario-cedes-centre-stage-to-a-thriving-west-census-shows/article2331829/?service=mobile (Sept. 6, 2012).

Gauthier, Pascal. 2011. "TD Special Report: Interprovincial Migration: Where Are Canadians Headed?" January 27. http://www.td.com/document/PDF/econo-mics/special/td-economics-special-pg0111-migration.pdf (January 27, 2011).

Gibbins, Roger. 1982. *Regionalism: Territorial Politics in Canada and the United States*. Toronto: Butterworths.

Gibbins, Roger, and Loleen Berdahl. 2003. *Western Visions, Western Futures: Perspectives on the West in Canada*. Peterborough, ON: Broadview Press.

Gidengil, Elisabeth, André Blais, Richard Nadeau, and Neil Nevitte. 1999. "Making Sense of Regional Voting in the 1997 Canadian Federal Election: Liberal and Reform Support Outside Quebec." *Canadian Journal of Political Science* 32 (2): 247–72. http://dx.doi.org/10.1017/S0008423900010489.

Gladwell, Malcolm. 2000. *The Tipping Point*. New York: Little Brown & Company.

Goerzen, Matt. 2010. "Absence Veiled Show of Support for Labour." *Brandon Sun,* May 15. http://www.brandonsun.com/opinion/absence-veiled-show-of-support-for-labour-93836459.html?path=/opinion&id=93836459&sortBy=oldest&view AllComments=y (May 15, 2010).

Goldfarb, Martin. 1977. *The Searching Nation: A Study of Canadians' Attitudes to the Future of Confederation.* Toronto: Southam Press.

Grenier, Eric. 2012. "NDP Wave's Next Destination May Be B.C., Polls Suggest." *Huffington Post Canada,* May 8. http://www.huffingtonpost ca/2012/05/08/ ndp-bc-polls-federal_n_1499365.html (November 16, 2012).

Hale, Geoffrey. 2006. *Uneasy Partnership: The Politics of Business and Government in Canada.* Peterborough, ON: Broadview Press.

Harrington, Carol. 2000. "Trudeau and Western Canada." *The Canadian Press,* September 29.

Head, Keith, and John Ries. 2010. "Do Trade Missions Increase Trade?" *Canadian Journal of Economics/Revue Canadienne d'Economique* 43 (3): 754–75. http:// dx.doi.org/10.1111/j.1540-5982.2010.01593.x.

Henderson, Alisa. 2004. "Regional Political Cultures in Canada." *Canadian Journal of Political Science* 37 (3): 595–615. http://dx.doi.org/10.1017/ S0008423904030707.

Hirsch, Todd. 2013. "Economic Truth: Alberta's Not Here for Itself Alone." *Globe and Mail,* January 14. http://www.theglobeandmail.com/commentary/economic-truth-albertas-not-here-for-itself-alone/article7263013/ (August 26, 2013).

Holden, Michael. 2012. *Who Cares about Baskets? We've Got Eggs! Diversification and Western Canada's Economic Future.* Calgary: Canada West Foundation.

Howard, Cosmo. 2011. "Under Harper, It's Tight Lips That Build Ships." *Globe and Mail,* October 25. http://www.theglobeandmail.com/news/politics/ under-harper-its-tight-lips-that-build-ships/article558794/ (October 25, 2011).

Hume, Mark. 2013. "Coal-shipment Permit Rocks Environmentalists." *Globe and Mail,* January 24. http://www.theglobeandmail.com/news/british-columbia/ vancouver-coal-shipment-permit-rocks-environmentalists/article7832279/ (August 26, 2013).

Hunter, Justine. 2013. "Clark: 'We Don't Need Alberta.'" *Globe and Mail,* May 6. http://www.theglobeandmail.com/news/british-columbia/we-dont-need-alberta-clark-pushes-natural-gas-as-key-to-bcs-success/article11729715/ (August 26, 2013).

Ibbitson, John. 2012. "The Collapse of the Laurentian Consensus: On the Westward Shift of Canadian Power and Values." December 5. http://reviewcanada.ca/ essays/2012/01/01/the-collapse-of-the-laurentian-consensus/ (May 26, 2013).

Internal Trade Secretariat. 2012. *Agreement on Internal Trade: Consolidated Version.* Winnipeg: Industry Canada.

Janigan, Mary. 2012. *Let the Eastern Bastards Freeze in the Dark: The West Versus the Rest since Confederation.* Toronto: Alfred A. Knopf.

Justice Canada. 2001. Immigration and Refugee Protection Act (S.C. 2001,c. 27). 12:1–3. http://laws-lois.justice.gc.ca/eng/acts/I-2.5/ (May 26, 2012).

Kennedy, Mark. 2012. "Foreign Buyouts Lack Public Support." *Calgary Herald,* December 19. http://www2.canada.com/calgaryherald/news/story. html?id=525cf6ee-4f1d-4da2-95e2-a34fbdae45ec&p=1 (December 19, 2012).

Kirby, Jason. 2010. "The Manitoba Miracle." *Maclean's,* December 6. http:// www2.macleans.ca/2010/12/06/the-manitoba-miracle/ (August 26, 2013).

Leach, Richard H. 1959. "Interprovincial Co-operation: Neglected Aspect of Canadian Federalism." *Canadian Public Administration* 2 (2): 83–99. http:// dx.doi.org/10.1111/j.1754-7121.1959.tb00543.x.

Leuprecht, Christian. 2003. "The Tory Fragment in Canada: Endangered Species?" *Canadian Journal of Political Science* 36 (2): 401–16. http://dx.doi.org/10.1017/S000842390377869X.

Lower, A.R.M. 1946. *From Colony to Nation: A History of Canada.* Toronto: Longmans, Green and Company.

Lu, Vanessa. 2013 "Toronto's Economy Forecast to Grow at 2.8 Per Cent in 2013." *Toronto Star,* February 14. http://www.thestar.com/business/economy/2013/02/14/torontos_economic_forecast_looks_strong_thank_the_us.html (February 14, 2012).

Mallory, J.R. 1953. *Social Credit and the Federal Power in Canada.* Toronto: University of Toronto Press.

Mamak, Alisa. 2012. "Census 2011 Interactive: Canada's West Grows as the East Stalls." *Globe and Mail,* February 8. http://www.theglobeandmail.com/news/national/census-2011-interactive-canadas-west-grows-as-the-east-stalls/article544500/ (June 18, 2012).

Martin, Don. 2002. "Your Tax Dollars at Work." *Calgary Herald,* May 7, A3.

Martin, Don. 2010. "What I Learned from 32 Years in the Newspaper Business." *National Post,* December 11. http://fullcomment.nationalpost.com/2010/12/11/don-martin-what-i-learned-from-32-years-in-the-newspaper-business/ (November 16, 2012).

McInnes, Craig. 2013. "Is Our Port Becoming a Locked Gateway?" *Vancouver Sun*, February 4. http://www2.canada.com/vancouversun/news/story.html?id=774ff6c6-b70b-4585-b2df-b163b306df87 (August 26, 2013).

Meekison, J. Peter. 2004a. "The Western Premiers' Conference: Intergovernmental Co-operation at the Regional Level." In *Canada: The State of the Federation 2002: Reconsidering the Institutions of Canadian Federalism,* ed. J. Peter Meekison, Hamish Telford, and Harvey Lazar, 183–209. Montreal: McGill-Queen's University Press.

Meekison, J. Peter. 2004b. "The Annual Premiers' Conference: Forging a Common Front." In *Canada: The State of the Federation 2002: Reconsidering the Institutions of Canadian Federalism,* ed. J. Peter Meekison, Hamish Telford, and Harvey Lazar, 141–82. Montreal: McGill-Queen's University Press.

Mehler Paperly, Anna. 2011. "Saskatoon Bound: Newcomers Lead Westward Shift." *Globe and Mail,* December 20. http://www.theglobeandmail.com/news/politics/saskatoon-bound-newcomers-lead-westward-shift/article4181602/ (June 22, 2012).

Mendelsohn, Matthew, and Sujit Choudhry. 2011. *Voter Equality and Other Canadian Values: Finding the Balance.* Toronto: Mowatt Centre for Policy Innovation.

Milan, Anne. 2011a. *Migration: International 2009.* Ottawa: Ministry of Industry.

Milan, Anne. 2011b. *Migration: Interprovincial 2008/2009.* Ottawa: Statistics Canada.

Morton, W.L. 1970. "The Bias of Prairie Politics." In *Historical Essays on the Prairie Provinces*, ed. Donald Swainson, 289–300. Toronto: McClelland and Stewart.

Murphy, Rex. 2012. "Peter Lougheed Was the Perfect Premier for Province Coming into Its Own." *National Post,* September 14. http://fullcomment.nationalpost.com/2012/09/14/rex-murphy-peter-lougheed-was-perfect-premier-for-province-coming-into-its-own/ (September 14, 2012).

O'Neill, Brenda, and Lynda Erickson. 2003. "Evaluating Traditionalism in the Atlantic Provinces: Voting, Public Opinion and the Electoral Project." *Atlantis: Critical Studies in Gender, Culture, and Social Justice* 27 (2): 113–29.

Ornstein, Michael D., H. Michael Stevenson, and A. Paul Williams. 1980. "Region, Class and Political Culture in Canada." *Canadian Journal of Political Science* 13 (2): 227–71. http://dx.doi.org/10.1017/S000842390003300X.

Owram, Doug. 2012. "Peter Lougheed Personified Rise of the New West." *Toronto Star,* September 15. http://www.thestar.com/opinion/editorialopinion/ 2012/09/15/peter_lougheed_personified_rise_of_the_new_west.html (November 19, 2012).

Pelletier, Réjean. 2002. "Intergovernmental Cooperation Mechanisms: Factors for Change?" *Commission on the Future of Health Care in Canada,* Discussion Paper No. 29. Ottawa: Royal Commission on the Future of Health Care in Canada. http://www.publications.gc.ca/collections/Collection/CP32-79-29-2002E.pdf (August 26, 2013).

Picot, Garnett. 2011. *Immigrant Economic and Social Outcomes in Canada: Research and Data Development at Statistics Canada.* Ottawa: Statistics Canada.

Pitts, Gordon. 2008. *Stampede! The Rise of the West and Canada's New Power Elite.* Toronto: Key Porter Books.

Pitts, Gordon. 2011. "An Educated Eye on Alberta's Future." *Globe and Mail,* June 20. http://www.theglobeandmail.com/report-on-business/careers/ careers-leadership/mike-percy-an-educated-eye-on-albertas-future/article 586303/ (August 26, 2013).

Prepost, Matt. 2010. "Immigrants Can Dodge Pitfalls." *Winnipeg Free Press,* October 2. http://www.winnipegfreepress.com/local/immigrants-can-dodge-pitfalls-104200359.html (October 2, 2010).

Press, Jordan. 2012. "BC and Alberta Growth Lead to Rise in West; Saskatchewan Sees Turnaround." *National Post,* February 8. http://news.nationalpost. com/2012/02/08/b-c-and-alberta-growth-lead-to-rise-in-west-saskatchewan-sees-turnaround/ (February 8, 2012).

Ramlo, Andrew, Ryan Berlin, and David Baxter. 2009. *Canada to 2058: Projections of Demographic Growth & Change for Canada and Its Regions.* Vancouver: Urban Future Institute.

Reid, John. 1993. "The 1970's: Sharpening the Sceptical Edge." In *The Atlantic Provinces in Confederation,* ed. E.R. Forbes and D.A. Muise, 460–504. Toronto: University of Toronto Press.

Resnick, Phillip. 2000. *The Politics of Resentment: British Columbia Regionalism and Canadian Unity.* Vancouver: UBC·Press.

Roach, Robert. 2003. *Common Ground: The Case for Interprovincial Cooperation in Western Canada.* Calgary: Canada West Foundation.

Roach, Robert. 2010. *State of the West 2010.* Ottawa: Department of Western Economic Diversification Canada.

Sancton, Andrew, and School of Public Policy & Governance. 2010. *The Principle of Representation by Population in Canadian Federal Politics.* Toronto: University of Toronto.

Savoie, Donald. 2000. "All Things Canadian Are Now Regional." *Journal of Canadian Studies/Revue d'Etudes Canadiennes* 35 (1): 203–17.

Savoie, Donald. 2003. *Reviewing Canada's Regional Development Efforts.* Ottawa: Royal Commission on Renewing and Strengthening Our Place in Canada.

Scarfe, Brian L. 1981. "The Federal Budget and Energy Program, October 28th, 1980: A Review." *Canadian Public Policy* 7 (1): 1–14. http://dx.doi. org/10.2307/3549850.

Scharpf, Fritz W. 1988. "The Joint-Decision Trap: Lessons from German Federalism and European Integration." *Public Administration* 66 (3): 239–78. http://dx.doi. org/10.1111/j.1467-9299.1988.tb00694.x.

Schwartz, Mildred. 1974. *Politics and Territory: The Sociology of Regional Persistence in Canada.* Montreal: McGill-Queen's University Press.

Simeon, Richard, and David Cameron. 2002. "Intergovernmental Relations and Democracy: An Oxymoron If There Ever Was One?" In *Canadian Federalism:*

Performance, Effectiveness, and Legitimacy, ed. Herman Bakvis and Grace Skogstad, 278–95. Don Mills, Ontario: Oxford University Press.

Simeon, R., and D.J. Elkins. 1974. "Regional Political Cultures in Canada." *Canadian Journal of Political Science* 7 (3): 397–437. http://dx.doi.org/10.1017/S0008423900040713.

Simeon, R., and D.J. Elkins. 1980. "Provincial Political Cultures in Canada." In *Small Worlds: Provinces and Parties in Canadian Political Life*, ed. D.J. Elkins and R. Simeon, 31–76. Toronto: Methuen.

Simeon, Richard. 2001. "Adaptability and Change in Federations." *International Social Science Journal* 53 (167): 145–52. http://dx.doi.org/10.1111/1468-2451.00303.

Simmons, Julie M. 2004. "Securing the Threads of Co-operation in the Tapestry of Intergovernmental Relations: Does the Institutionalization of Ministerial Conferences Matter?" In *Canada: The State of the Federation 2002: Reconsidering the Institutions of Canadian Federalism*, ed. J. Peter Meekison, Hamish Telford, and Harvey Lazar, 285–311. Montreal: McGill-Queen's University Press.

Smiley, Donald. 1976. *Canada in Question: Federalism in the Seventies*. 2nd ed. Toronto: McGraw-Hill.

Smith, David. 1976. "The Prairie Provinces." In *The Provincial Political Systems: Comparative Essays*, ed. David J. Bellamy, Jon H. Pammett, and Donald C. Rowat, 46–61. Toronto: Methuen.

Smith, Denis. 1970. "Liberals and Conservatives on the Prairies, 1917–1968." In *Prairie Perspectives*, ed. David P. Gagan, 30–44. Toronto: Holt, Rinehart and Winston.

Soroka, Stuart, Richard Johnston, and Keith Banting. 2007. "Ties That Bind? Social Cohesion and Diversity in Canada." In *Belonging? Diversity, Recognition and Shared Citizenship in Canada*, ed. Keith Banting, Thomas Courchene, and F. Leslie Seidle, 1–40. Montreal: Institute for Research on Public Policy.

Stanley, Della. 1993. "The 1960's: The Illusions and Realities of Progress." In *The Atlantic Provinces in Confederation*, ed. E.R Forbes and D.A Muise, 421–59. Toronto: University of Toronto Press.

Statistics Canada. 2009. *Births*. Ottawa: Ministry of Industry.

Statistics Canada. 2010. "Observed (2009) and Projected (2036) Population According to Three Scenarios, Canada, Provinces, and Territories." July 5. http://www.statcan.gc.ca/daily-quotidien/100526/t100526b1-eng.htm (August 2, 2013).

Statistics Canada. 2012a. "Labour Force Characteristics, Seasonally Adjusted, By Province (Monthly)." http://www.statcan.gc.ca/tables-tableaux/sum-som/l01/cst01/lfss01b-eng.htm (May 26, 2013).

Statistics Canada. 2012b. "CANSIM Table 029–0005 Capital Expenditures By Sector, By Province and Territory." http://www.statcan.gc.ca/tables-tableaux/sum-som/l01/cst01/busi03a-eng.htm (May 26, 2013).

Statistics Canada. 2012c. *The Canadian Population in 2011: Population Counts and Growth*. Ottawa: Ministry of Industry.

Statistics Canada. 2012d. *The Canadian Population in 2011: Age and Sex*. Ottawa: Ministry of Industry.

Statistics Canada. 2012e. "Age and Sex Highlight Tables, 2011 Census, Table 2: Population by Broad Age Groups and Sex, Counts, Including Median Age, 1921 to 2011 for Both Sexes." https://www12.statcan.gc.ca/census-recensement/2011/dp-pd/hlt-fst/as-sa/Pages/highlight.cfm?TabID=1&Lang=E&PRCode=01&Asc=0&OrderBy=1&Sex=1&View=1&tableID=22 (July 25, 2012).

Statistics Canada. 2012f. *Education Indicators in Canada: An International Perspective*. Ottawa: Canadian Education Statistics Council.

Statistics Canada. 2012g. "Dependency Ratio: 2006 Census and Administrative Data by Age Group for July 1, Canada, Provinces, Territories, Health Regions: 2011 Boundaries and Peer Groups." http://www5.statcan.gc.ca/cansim/pick-choisir?id=1095326&p2=20&retrLang=eng&lang=eng (May 24, 2012).

Statistics Canada. 2013a. "Aboriginal Peoples in Canada: First Nations People, Métis and Inuit." http://www12.statcan.gc.ca/nhs-enm/2011/as-sa/99-011-x/99-011-x2011001-eng.cfm (May 23, 2013).

Statistics Canada. 2013b. "Immigration and Ethnocultural Diversity in Canada." http://www12.statcan.gc.ca/nhs-enm/2011/as-sa/99-010-x/99-010-x2011001-eng.cfm (May 23, 2013).

Statistics Canada. 2013c. *Focus on Geography Series.* http://www12.statcan.gc.ca/nhs-enm/2011/as-sa/fogs-spg/Pages/ProvinceSelector.cfm?lang=E&level=2 (May 23, 2013).

Statistics Canada. 2013d. *Mother Tongue (percentage distribution), Canada, Provinces and Territories, 2011 Census.* http://www12.statcan.gc.ca/census-recensement/lang-tab-eng.cfm#note1 (May 23, 2013).

Taber, Jane. 2011. "Harper's Team Keeps Hands Off $35-Billion Shipbuilding Hot Potato." *Globe and Mail,* October 17. http://www.theglobeandmail.com/news/politics/ottawa-notebook/harpers-team-keeps-hands-off-35-billion-shipbuilding-hot-potato/article618407/ (October 17, 2011).

Taber, Jane. 2012. "Equalization and EI Hurt Saskatchewan, Premier Says." *Globe and Mail.* January 10. http://www.theglobeandmail.com/news/politics/ottawa-notebook/equalization-and-ei-hurt-saskatchewan-premier-says/article542474/ (January 10, 2012).

Tajfel, Henri, Michael Billig, Robert Bundy, and Claude Flament. 1971. "Social Categorization and Intergroup Behavior." *European Journal of Social Psychology* 1 (2): 149–78. http://dx.doi.org/10.1002/ejsp.2420010202.

The Economist. 2012. "Canada's Economy: A Two-Speed North." *The Economist,* March 31. http://www.economist.com/blogs/americasview/2012/03/canadas-economy (March 31, 2012).

Thorburn, H.G. 1984. *Planning and the Economy: Building Federal-Provincial Consensus.* Toronto: James Lorimer & Company.

Tomblin, Stephen G. 1995. *Ottawa and the Outer Provinces: The Challenge of Regional Integration in Canada.* Toronto: James Lorimer & Company.

Tomblin, Stephen G. 2007. "Effecting Change and Transformation through Regionalization: Theory versus Practice." *Canadian Public Administration* 50 (1): 1–20. http://dx.doi.org/10.1111/j.1754-7121.2007.tb02000.x.

Turner, John C. 1978. "Social Comparison, Similarity and In-group Favoritism." In *Differentiation between Social Groups: Studies in the Social Psychology of Intergroup Relations,* ed. H. Tajfel, 235–50. London: Academic Press.

Underhill, Frank H. 1960. *In Search of Canadian Liberalism.* Toronto: Macmillan.

Urban Futures Institute. 2008. *Dimension of Diversity: 2006 Census Snapshot. Diversity in Location: Our Urban and Rural Portrait.* Vancouver: Urban Futures Institute.

Vancouver Sun. 2012. "Census 2011—The Rise of Western Canada (Video)." http://www.canada.com/news/2011-census/Census+video+rise+Western+Canada/6119897/story.html (June 20, 2012).

Van Biesebroeck, Johannes, Emily Yu, and Shenjie Chen. 2010. "The Impact of Trade Promotion Services on Canadian Exporter Performance." Presented at the Forum for Research in Empirical International Trade, Working Paper #184. http://dx.doi.org/10.2139/ssrn.1612209.

Vanderklippe, Nathan. 2013. "An Energy Bridge to BC's Cost: Leading Aboriginal Entrepreneurs Team Up to Help Push for Pipelines." *Globe and Mail,* February 5.

Wall, Brad, Ed Stelmach, and Gordon Campbell. 2010. "We Are Stronger as One than if We Stand Apart." *Globe and Mail,* May. http://www.theglobeandmail.com/commentary/we-are-stronger-as-one-than-if-we-stand-apart/article1210958/ (May 26, 2013).

Wesley, Jared J. 2011. *Code Politics: Campaigns and Cultures on the Canadian Prairies.* Vancouver: UBC Press.

Western Concept Party. 1993. "Pat Burns Editorial, CJOR Radio Vancouver, November 10, 1986." *The Western Separatist Papers* (September): 3.

Western Economic Diversification Canada. 2009. "Western Canada's Economic Environment." http://www.wd.gc.ca/eng/10263.asp (May 26, 2013).

Western Economic Diversification Canada. 2012. "The Department." October 24. http://www.wd.gc.ca/eng/36.asp (May 26, 2013).

Wingrove, Josh, Dawn Walton, and Carrie Tait. 2012. "Tributes Pour in For Peter Lougheed." *Globe and Mail,* September 13. http://www.theglobeandmail.com/news/national/tributes-pour-in-for-peter-lougheed/article4544459/ (September 13, 2012).

Wood, James. 2013. "Redford Says Cuts to Come Quickly." *Calgary Herald,* January 15. http://www2.canada.com/calgaryherald/news/story.html?id=592be8e5-fcc2-40be-b7e8-bde59e13406b (August 26, 2013).

Yukon, Northwest Territories, and Nunavut. 2007. *A Northern Vision: A Stronger North and a Better Canada.* http://www.anorthernvision.ca/pdf/backgroundnorthernvision_en.pdf (May 26, 2013).

Zhao, Jun, Li Xue, and Tara Gilkinson. 2010. *Health Status and Social Capital of Recent Immigrations in Canada: Evidence from the Longitudinal Survey of Immigrants to Canada.* Ottawa: Citizenship and Immigration Canada.

Zimmerman, Joseph. 1996. *Interstate Relations: The Neglected Dimension of Federalism.* Westport, CT: Praeger.

Zimmerman, Joseph. 2002. *Interstate Cooperation: Compacts and Administrative Agreements.* Westport, CT: Praeger.

Index